Seduced into Shame

Finding Freedom from Sexual Sins

LAURA GAGNON

Seduced into Shame

ACKNOWLEDGEMENT

I would like to acknowledge my utmost gratitude to several people whose wisdom, encouragement and feedback helped to greatly enrich the content of this book.

First, to my husband Norm, whose constant love and support of my writing give me the confidence to share such important truths to the body of Christ. His thoughts, pastoral experience, and spiritual insights are vital components on this topic and are also incorporated into this book.

Secondly, to Pastor Bill Burkhardt, who is an amazing friend and support to our family as well as so many others. His insights on the topic of spiritual identity are valuable and greatly needed in the body of Christ. It is my pleasure to include a chapter written by Bill expressing life in Christ from the perspective of a new identity.

Lastly, I would like to express my thanks to a very gifted Christian minister and professional Theophostic counselor, Mrs. Shelly Royalty. The way she has learned to partner with the Holy Spirit to release healing to others is profound and effective, and provides a better approach to ministry. Some of her counsel is also shared in this book. I am grateful to learn from Shelly and call her my friend.

CONTENTS

PREFACE

It is an awesome privilege to minister and share the words of healing and deliverance that has been given by the Holy Spirit and His servant, Laura Gagnon.

Out of her personal testimony and walk with Jesus she shares the intimacy and depths of freedom from the demonic strongholds that have plagued the church and every believer since creation. The words you are about to read are powerful and cuts to the root of oppressive thoughts stemming from lust and shame. It is the Lord's will that all his children experience true freedom from sexual sins, captivating thoughts, condemning mindsets, and broken shame in this lifetime. Freedom is not afforded to just the few but for all who call on his name.

Laura has prayed and petitioned the Lord about how to draw people into the subject matter, as well as the challenge of leading people to read and understand the principles laid out in this book.

Many people are wounded and shamed by religious judgement and accusations. They have been hiding and keeping their secret in fear of rejection and condemnation.

This book is not the final answer but the beginning of breaking down the walls of fear; for it's by faith in God's promises and understanding of the enemies tactics and strategies that freedom is seen and fulfilled.

Please take the time to prayerfully read over every chapter. The prayers and declarations will have spiritual and eternal repercussions, both for the kingdom benefit and the enemy's dismay.

Norm Gagnon

FORWARD

"Just as He chose us in Him before the foundation of the world, that we should be holy and without blame before Him in love, having predestined us to adoption as sons..." (Ephesians 1:4-5)

God's core desire for creation was to have children (sons). As a Father, God's love motivated Him to enjoy unbroken relationship with His kids. He adopts us into His family, and fully accepts us as His own children (Eph. 1:5). The Godhead is a safe place for you and I to discover acceptance.

God chose us to be "holy and without blame" before Him (Eph. 4). "Without blame" means free from shame. God designed you and I to be thoroughly free from shame. Adam and Eve enjoyed relationship with God in the garden in a state where they were "naked and not ashamed" (Gen. 2:25).

God wants interaction with His kids without any hindrance or obstacle. Therefore, God will aggressively identify and remove anything that interferes with His relationship with His kids. No obstacle will remain standing that keeps God from His kids - and this includes shame.

God knew that Adam's fall would change Adam's view of himself. God the Father knew Adam would feel unrighteous and ashamed rather than "holy and without blame". Adam's awareness of his unrighteousness and the corresponding shame he felt inspired him to hide from God. Shame changes our view of ourselves in a way that interferes with our relationship with God.

Adam's sin separated Him from God from man's point of view, but didn't separate God from man from God's point of view. Adam was moving away from God, focused on His sin and shame. But God was moving toward Adam, bringing His effective remedy for sin and shame.

The coat of animal skin God provided for Adam pointed forward to the perfect sacrifice of Christ that would remove our sin and shame. Now in Christ, we are "holy and without blame and totally free from condemnation (Rom. 8:1).

Because God accepts us, He has freed us from the fear of rejection that an orphan feels. An orphan is often ashamed of who they are. They wonder, "Why was I rejected by my own parents?"

"For you did not receive the spirit of bondage again to fear, but you received the Spirit of adoption by whom we cry out, "Abba, Father." (Romans 8:15-16)

God is determined to destroy the tormenting fear of rejection that affects the human race. The "Spirit of Adoption" replaces our orphan mentality with the comforting knowledge of God's acceptance.

Imagine yourself being enveloped in acceptance by the Godhead: The Father loves you, the Holy Spirit helps you understand your value, and Jesus would rather die than live without you! Heaven's healthy family is God's destination point for every one of earth's shame-filled orphans!

God wants you free of shame, but Satan, as the accuser of the brethren, works full time to get people mired in a swamp of condemnation and shame.

Laura Gagnon has written this book as a manual to help you live shame-free. Several of her chapters are devoted to helping you identify areas where shame may have gained a foothold in your life. Laura has also included some prayers to help you live completely free of shame. So, enjoy God's invitation to live shame-free!

Pastor Bill Burkhardt

Lifegate Church, Encinitas, CA

INTRODUCTION

Multitudes of people have felt lost, frustrated and have borne the stigma of feeling like an outcast for far too long. There are lost sheep that have been wandering on the hills of hopelessness and despair, separated from the rest of the flock. There are others that are within the flock that feel just as alone, as if they were outside the camp, because internally they carry the weight of guilt, condemnation and shame. They go to church, put on a smiling face and pretend that all is well. They are the walking wounded. These people are all around us, and many that we would never suspect are living with secret shame. Even children are not exempt. The enemy is no respecter of people. Young and old alike of every background, nationality, profession and gender suffer under his oppression. He tempts, entices, ensnares and chains his victims to bondage and fear. If the enemy has you chained, branded with dishonor and fear of disgrace, then you are not alone.

When the enemy leaves his mark on people, it is to create negative cycles in their life so that they receive more and more rejection, fear and shame. It is to isolate them from fellowship and intimacy in relationships so that those individuals remain broken and in bondage. The enemy's mark upon a person is to brand them as an outcast so that others will continue to see them as unclean. It releases a shunning spirit over them, so that others will continue to see them through the lens of rejection. The intent from the enemy is to cause people to lose their voice and credibility, their ability to move forward and fulfill their destiny. It brings such heaviness that it leaves people in a state of hopelessness. It is like forcing them to wear garments of shame for their entire life. This greatly devalues a person and hangs over them as a curse in the spirit realm.

So many people are bound with their head bowed, as if they were put in stocks. In ancient Roman times, prisoners would be thrown in the deepest, darkest pit of the prison, an area that was reserved for the vilest outcasts. Their head, hands and feet were fastened in a wooden frame that left them completely unable to stand upright and with very little room for movement. They were chained and padlocked inside the stocks as punishment. Although many awaited trial, most simply awaited their death.

A Christian that is bound with shame is like a person that has allowed the enemy to put them in stocks. Satan's delight is to feel that he is our owner and master; and that he has the keys to our freedom. He wants us to believe that he holds the keys to our future. Yet, the truth of the matter is that Jesus Christ has left the keys in our hands. God's will is never for people to live in shame. Our shepherd is sympathetic and tender towards those that have been abused, rejected and branded by the enemy. He understands the pain of rejection, the cruelty of the adversary, and the horrific wounds that are caused by humiliation. He is a compassionate Healer. Satan has long been aware of the power of shame as a tool of destruction. The enemy's attempt to besmirch people with a permanent black mark upon their life and destiny are graciously and permanently removed through the victory available in Christ Jesus.

"I am the LORD your God, who brought you out of Egypt so that you would no longer be slaves to the Egyptians; I broke the bars of your yoke and enabled you to walk with heads held high." (Leviticus 26:13, NIV)

Both my husband and I struggled under the enemy's oppression for many years, and we understand what it feels like to be bound. It is being trapped in your own personal prison. Fear and shame will isolate a person from others. Demonic attachments and generational curses caused pain and contributed to failures. The hurt and shame over some of those events caused such mental and emotional pain that it seemed at times as though it was difficult to ever find real healing and freedom.

In this day and age it seems that there is a crowd of people who are out there lurking, waiting to be offended. And when they are, they immediately take to social media to promulgate their offense, using the weapon of shame against those they scorn. The very sad reality is that fear causes anger, defensiveness and sometimes violence. They are the byproducts of shame, because a person feels a deep need to somehow restore their self-image. The need to restore self-esteem is also a driving force behind living in pretense. The fear of man is so strong that it causes people to project a fake persona; others will never truly know the real person behind the mask. Fear of judgment and disgrace seems to hang in the air as an unseen influence. That influence constantly reminds us that to admit weakness or failure is making oneself vulnerable, and no one wants to appear vulnerable to a world that loves to shame people at whim. Those unspoken thoughts and feelings makes it even more difficult for people to ask for help when they do have a problem.

Writing this book was not necessarily something I wanted to do, simply due to the nature of the subject matter. It is no easy thing to bare one's soul to the world in utter transparency. Yet, time and time again, I continue to receive correspondence from those that have read articles on my blog, asking for help. Allow me to share a portion of one person's correspondence, if you will, because this person's words describe the nature of the problem. *"I've asked many preachers for help. I've been to multiple 'deliverance services' to see if I can find freedom from this problem...Nothing has been successful. Everyone I ask for help treats me as if I have the plague. When I tell them the problem they won't talk to me again. It is really a horrible problem when you can't even get help from the church."*

90% of the people who contact me on the subject of sexual demons and addictions voice the same kind of situations. What is equally frustrating are those who write or teach others on spiritual matters, telling them such things like incubus or succubus spirits do not exist, when they have no actual experience on the subject. Just because something may not be understood by some people doesn't mean it doesn't exist. There are those, like myself, who have seen, felt, battled and wrestled with these demonic spirits. It is very hurtful and harmful for anyone to tell them that what they have experienced isn't real. Many people have turned to traditional forms of counseling for help but have not found any peace, remedy or answers.

Pastors and ministry leaders have a lot on their plate. It's reasonable that they might feel overwhelmed. People often fear what they don't understand, but it's also obvious that something needs to be fixed. The kind of situation I described ought to convict the heart of every Christian. We must stop shooting the wounded and start lifting up and encouraging our brothers and sisters. God calls us to war, but not against one another. We are in the same army! It's time for us to come alongside our brothers and sisters and tell them, *"We're going to help you. We'll go to war with you to see these things defeated, and we won't stop until every enemy is dead. You are not unclean and rejected. We will pray that mark of shame off of you. We accept you and we are here to help."*

I have come to realize that there were reasons why I went through the things I experienced. I lived with those spirits for decades before I got free, and others can benefit from what I have learned. From the very beginning of my life, the enemy had marked me as an outcast. He did everything possible to insure that I would never find my voice, or my place within the body of Christ. Perhaps in reading this book others will find some of those truths ringing loud and clear about their own lives. If so, then this book is full of insights so that you, too, can obtain your freedom.

Practical steps to freedom are included so that people

can learn how to be effective in working through issues in their own life, as well as learn how to equip others.

Scripture tells us that people are destroyed for lack of knowledge. The enemy counts on people being ignorant of his ways. That is why it is so crucial to anyone seeking genuine healing and restoration to learn what God has said in His word, and to discern good from evil. My hope is to help educate others about an area of healing ministry that is rarely talked about, and few seem to understand. There are spiritually rooted issues tied into lust and sexual sins that must be addressed if people are to get free!

This is a message that can easily be seen as one that will bring healing to the heart of the church. Shame is a byproduct of living under condemnation, but through a life in Christ, all of that guilt, condemnation and shame can be broken. When the power of fear and shame are broken, it releases faith to live without the mask of pretense, pride and insecurity. The person is released into the life Christ has called us to: a greater level of empathy, humility and transparency. It is my delight to expose the works of darkness and the deception of the enemy just as much as it is to share insights with others about the heart of God. Once people know the truth, the truth can set them free.

One of the victories that lies ahead of anyone that has been attacked by the enemy is retribution. It's payback for all the trouble they've had to go through. Christ's victory became mine, and now my victory (through my testimony and teaching) can become your victory. It is the transforming power of God's grace working to bring healing and transformation.

Take heart, my friend, for God knows the questions of your heart and He is here to provide answers. It is my sincere hope and desire that you find the answers that are needed to help you regain your freedom. I have no doubt that if you follow the godly counsel within these pages, you will encounter Jesus our Liberating King. I pray that you shake off the chains that have had you bound! May you recover your voice, find your place in the body of Christ and fulfill all your purpose. Within these pages you will discover the Lord who lovingly places your face in His hands and smiles upon you. Jesus is the ultimate **SHAME BREAKER**.

CHAPTER 1

BOUND BY SHAME

God's plan from the beginning was to have sons and daughters so that He could have relationship with mankind. His motive was not to have servants, but children with whom He could share His heart in unbroken fellowship. When He created Adam and Eve and set them in the garden of paradise, it was because He desired intimacy in relationship.

God made Adam first, then took a rib out of Adam's side and made him a wife. They were made for one another. Their hearts were pure and innocent, because from the beginning they were made to have intimate fellowship with God. Scripture says,

"And the man and his wife were both naked and were not ashamed." Genesis 2:25 ESV)

Imagine the awe and wonder of giving birth to a long awaited child, and the fullness of joy that is felt in holding that baby, gazing down upon his face. You are so full of love you feel your heart will burst. That is how God felt when He created Adam and Eve. His joy and delight in His creation was not diminished by the fact that they were fully mature. On the contrary, He could have meaningful conversation and relationship with them from the very beginning of their lives. He provided everything necessary for Adam and Eve to enjoy the beauty of the garden and a life of fulfillment. They lacked nothing. Every evening God would visit them and they would talk about their day. They would excitedly share all their new discoveries while He listened intently. Adam and Eve had His undivided attention and they flourished in His love. As their Father, He could hardly wait to spend time with his kids, and they equally valued their time with Him. That was their special time together.

Consider what it would be like to have unbroken communion with God. Our minds cannot even comprehend it! If I were Adam and Eve, I would not be able to contain myself waiting for Father to show up every evening. Like an excited child, I would run to the door to meet Him and jump all over Him, showering Him with hugs and kisses. I would be so excited and full of questions I would be bubbling over with anticipation. I doubt if I could think of anything else aside from wanting to be in His presence. And why not? The Father's presence is absolute pure love, acceptance and delight. He is not stuffy or emotionally disconnected from His kids. He loves us with a deep, everlasting, unconditional love. He shares in our enthusiasm for life and He laughs when we are silly. Now, imagine that you have enjoyed all that, truly delighting yourself in the Lord. And one day, quite unexpectedly, a stranger showed up with the insidious desire to destroy the love and bond that you shared not only with your Father, but your spouse. In one swift move by the enemy, a family is broken. This is what we walk into in Genesis chapter 3.

The intimacy in their relationship was interrupted by the lies whispered to Eve, from the one who despised her very existence: *the serpent.* Lucifer (also known as the devil and Satan) became jealous of this son and daughter because he saw that they had captured the heart of God.

Up until Adam and Eve came along, Lucifer felt special, and he was. He was extremely handsome in appearance. He was the seal of perfection, full of wisdom and covered in the rarest and most beautiful gems. Precious stones have no light of themselves. They can only reflect the light that shines upon them, and his was brilliant. He was known as the bright morning star because he reflected the glory of God. He, too, walked with God and enjoyed his fellowship. Ezekiel 28:14 says that he was the *anointed guardian cherub that covers*;

he was placed on the holy mountain of God. Cherubim are sometimes depicted as small chubby angels with a childlike face, but that is not accurate. They are actually described as quite formidable creatures in the book of Ezekiel.[1] They are created beings that protect the holy things of God. They guard God's domain from sin and corruption.[2] They are also symbolic of God's holy presence because they are always in His presence. Lucifer's role was not just as the worship leader in heaven, as is sometimes implied. He was an instrument to bring praise and glory to God. His voice was described as having a tabret and pipes, which are musical instruments. Worship was indeed a part of his role, but it was so much more than that. The way he was made was literally a form of praise to God because he was so beautiful, wise, equipped in melody and truly a sight to behold. He walked in the midst of the fiery stones that came from God's altar. He lived in the very presence of God. He was a guardian and protector of God's holiness and presence. Scripture tells us that Lucifer was "perfect in his ways from the day he was created – *until* iniquity was found in him."[3] That means that Lucifer at one point was blameless and morally pure. We know this is true because God does not allow sin or

---

[1] Ezekiel 1:1-24; 10:3-8, 10:12,14, 20-22.

[2] Psalm 80:1; Psalm 99:1

[3] Ezek. 28:15

corruption in heaven.

Even though he was the image of perfection and covered in every beautiful, precious stone imaginable, it was not enough. He was created in such perfection that even his wisdom was without fault. He was created holy and blameless, **until** he grew full of pride. He corrupted his wisdom and perfection for the sake of his splendor. The extent of his betrayal is incomprehensible. I cannot personally fathom how much pride and arrogance developed in him to lead him in such rebellion against God. He was in the presence of perfect love, acceptance and holiness from the very beginning of his creation, and yet he was willing to throw it all away. His lust was insatiable. Lucifer wanted to be like God and receive the worship that rightfully belonged to God. He wanted to be adored, like God. He wanted others to enthrone him and raise him up in power so that he could be a god. He wanted to be in charge, and fought for the right to live independently of God's will. Rules were for subordinates! He would do as he pleased. So God cast Lucifer to the ground, and a third of the angels who had followed him into rebellion fell with him.[4]

It is almost inconceivable that someone assigned such a

---

[4] Revelation 12:4, 7-9

an important role in heaven, living in constant fellowship with God and perfect in his ways could take such a turn for the worse. He willingly, maliciously broke God's trust. The extent of his betrayal is so deep it is abhorrent. Once cast out of heaven, every sense of moral purity and perfection was completely stripped away from him. Instead of being clothed in beauty, he became hideous to behold. He became known as Satan, the accuser. He exchanged the honor he had in heaven for dishonor and reproach, and he became clothed in condemnation, shame, rage and bitterness. His fate was sealed and the day of his eternal destruction awaited. Void of all love, he became full of fear, vengeance and hatred towards God.

Scripture is not clear as to the timing when Lucifer was expelled from heaven, but we do know it was prior to Genesis chapter 3 because the serpent, (also known as the deceiver, the devil and Satan), first appeared in the garden of Eden. Lucifer and the angels that fell with him did so some time after the original creation of the earth. My personal theory is that Lucifer became jealous of God's plan to bring forth mankind. He would never be a son of God and thus became discontent with the way God made him. And so, he conspired a reckless and arrogant plan to hold on to his esteemed position he had come to enjoy in heaven. He wanted to seize God's throne for himself and overthrow His authority. Out of this pride and rebellion, he conspired the plan to ruin the relationship Adam and Eve enjoyed with their father.

Satan, appearing as a serpent in the garden, was full of lust and covetousness, and full of hatred for God's true sons and daughters. With the utmost cunning and an acute sense of knowing precisely how to appeal to the woman, the evil one proceeded to weave his smooth sounding lies into a web of deception. He laid it all out before her with the suggestion – no, the *accusation* – that her Father was too restrictive. Satan's lie was that God didn't want Eve to enjoy fulfillment, and His boundaries were meant to deprive her of freedom. And when Eve listened, when she tempted Adam to also disobey God's command, both were immediately covered in fear, guilt and shame. When God came looking for them in the garden for His usual time of fellowship, Adam and Eve hid. They covered themselves in fig leaves to hide their nakedness, but it wasn't enough to cleanse the guilt and shame from their conscience. The first thing the enemy lost as a result of his pride was the first thing he went after in God's children: their purity. They, too, had also been created to be holy and blameless, to live in God's presence and enjoy His fellowship. If Satan couldn't enjoy God's presence any longer then neither would they! The whispers of temptation succeeded in breaking the bond of intimacy and trust between the Father and His children, and it broke all of their hearts.

As you can see, Satan's downfall was not just because of pride, but due to *lust* and *covetousness*. **The door to lust is not always through the things that people might expect.** Through the pages of this book we will explore the less obvious spiritual relationships between lust, temptation and the means by which Satan seduces people into making ungodly peace treaties. Every lie is tailored to appeal to his prey. Satan crafts the temptation in order to lead people into a snare. Once he has them hooked, he binds them to fear, pride and disgrace. Then the person begins to make fig leaves to cover their shame.

The enemy knows how to skillfully paint a picture of an unfair, restrictive and punitive God. The deceiver is the one who portrays a loving Father as one who stands watching over others, stick in hand, as nothing more than a harsh disciplinarian. It is the tempter that whispers, *"Go ahead, taste and see this is good. It won't harm you."* It almost sounds a bit like the same logic he used on Eve. All the while, he counters sound reason with the accusation that it's the Father who is trying to deprive people from experiencing the fullness of life. When people believe the lie, they accuse God of being overly rigid. They push away the conviction so that they can do as they please, and form an agreement with the accuser. "God *is* too rigid." "This won't hurt me." "I'll be careful. I won't get caught." Or, "I am old enough to make my own decisions. Stop trying to tell me what to do! I don't need a helicopter parent." And just like that, the wedge is driven deeper. Separation begins. It could be any number of thoughts that race through the mind in a matter of seconds. When people partner with the accuser, they don't even realize they've taken the bait the enemy has carefully placed before them. He dangles the thought in front of them again, . slowly reeling them in. When he has them in hand, then he can trip the trigger to their pride so that they blame God for being the source of the their perceived judgement and condemnation. When people wear garments of shame, they fight to recover what's been lost, but in their own strength. If people could only recognize the lie! Actually, the exact opposite is true.

"For God did not send the Son into the world to judge the world, but that the world might be saved through Him." (John 3:17)

The Father's plan has always been intimacy in relationship. That is why He sent His son as an ambassador of His kingdom. God's willingness to forgive us of our sins was made evident before Jesus ever went to the cross.

Countless people were touched by his love and compassion. Perhaps one of the greatest displays of the tender heart of our shepherd is seen in his interaction with the adulterous woman in John chapter eight.

Years of emotional pain were bottled up inside this woman. One lover after another used her, abused her and cast her aside. *"Unclean,"* they said. Her heart was torn, over and over again, every time another man rejected her and moved onto someone else. *Rejected.* The word hung around her like a heavy blanket of hopelessness. *Outcast.* Daily she heard the whispers of those who despised her, and saw the looks of disgust as they cast their eyes upon her in judgment. She had been branded with shame and bore the reputation as an adulterous women. These were the scars of her punishment, but the enemy wasn't finished with her yet. He figured he still needed her just a little longer, and had a plan to kill two birds with one stone. He would use her to take down the threat to his kingdom. Another carefully contrived plot emerged. He would catch her in the act and bring her before the townspeople where he could publicly accuse her. He would force Jesus into a corner, and then be able to bring charges against him for violating the law of Moses. It was a certain death penalty for both of them. Or so he thought.

When some of the people dragged the woman into the public square and threw her at the feet of Jesus, they demanded a response. "This woman was caught in the act of adultery!" They thought they could force Him to condemn her, yet the exact opposite occurred. He walked over to her and gazed down on her tear stained face, then looked upon the angry expressions of those that proudly exalted their judgments. Slowly, He stooped down and began to write words in the sand. No one really knows what He wrote. Perhaps they were the secret sins of those who accused her. Perhaps He wrote something like this:

"Who you are is not what do in public; it's what you are in private."

He looked up and glanced around at the angry mob. *"Let those who are without sin cast the first stone."* A heavy weight hung in the air. Tensions were high. Then, slowly, one by one the Pharisees dropped their stones and walked away as conviction gripped their hearts. They felt naked before Him. Who was this man who could see into their very soul? They hated him all the more, but left, fearful lest their own sins be exposed and brought into the light.

Jesus asked, *"Woman, where are your accusers? Did no one step forward to condemn you?"*

"I don't know," she whispered, unable to meet His gaze.

"Neither do I condemn you," He said. *"Go and sin no more."*

This woman was overcome by the intense fear of exposure. The shame of being publicly disgraced and looked down upon by others who felt secure in their judgments was the deepest wound she had ever experienced. *Outcast! Unloved. Expendable.* These labels would be forever etched into her mind. Yet, in the midst of her greatest pain and shame she met the most benevolent, gracious, kind individual she had ever encountered. Jesus restored her hope, and she would be forever grateful.

She wasn't the only one, of course. Lepers were cleansed. Demoniacs were set free. The woman with the issue of blood was healed. Multitudes who had been marked by the enemy as unclean and unable to find acceptance in society were transformed by an encounter with the Lord. Jesus' whole purpose was to demonstrate the reality of the kingdom of God and to reveal the heart of the Father to His people. Jesus frequently remarked, *"If you've seen Me, you've seen the Father."* He didn't come to judge people for their sin, but He did say that those that rejected His gracious offer to have their sins forgiven were already under the same condemnation as Satan. God is not surprised when people make wrong choices. He knows the enemy is constantly trying to turn people against Him, but those things never changed His course of action. Jesus came to remove the stain of guilt and demonstrate the gracious mercy of God.

Our Father knows that people want to live free from disgrace. No one has to live under a black cloud of guilt, condemnation and shame. Condemnation is the byproduct of shame, but scripture tells us that we have been emancipated from the death grip of sin **and** shame through Jesus Christ. We are no longer slaves of sin. The question is, which identity are you living in? The old man or the new man? If a person lives in the old identity, then there is a part of him that is chained to the old master, Satan. So, the key to understanding is why the chain to the old master is not yet broken. There is a part of that person that needs to die so that the new nature can take effect. We don't try to breathe life into the old man, because the old man has to die. But, when that person makes a choice to live in Christ, then a *new law* takes effect, and under that new law it is written in Romans 8:1, *"therefore, now no condemnation awaits those who are living in Jesus the Anointed, the Liberating King."* The law of the Spirit of Life breathes into them and liberates that person from the law of sin and death. The ability to live in our new nature is because we walk according to the movement of the Spirit in our lives. There are many people who understand these truths, yet continue to live chained as a slave to the enemy. The question in their minds are, "What am I missing?" "Why can I not seem to get the victory?" Read on, and I will show you.

No one has to live feeling defeated. Christ came as an answer for our sin issues. That is why He generously gave His own life as a love offering. Falsely accused, stripped, beaten, mocked and humiliated – Jesus hung naked on a cross as the sin and shame of the world was placed solely upon Him. He is well acquainted with shame because He was punished in our place. He was despised and rejected with such a vengeance, so covered in disgrace, that people hid their faces from him. It was *because* Jesus was punished in our place that He is able to completely forgive our sin and set us free. Why would He willingly take all that punishment upon himself only to punish us later for our sins? That would be completely illogical! That is why He said, "It is finished." The only one who has a legitimate right to condemn us has forgiven us.

Yet, the sad reality is many Christians continue to live in bondage because they're still believing the lies the enemy has told them. Unfortunate as it is, the church has, at times, reinforced the world's perspective of judgment and condemnation. If you are one who has experienced the rejection, judgement or condemnation from the body of Christ, I ask you to forgive us. I know how much it hurts. We have sinned in our judgments. We have sinned by not loving others with an unconditional love, and I'm sorry that we caused you to feel more pain and misunderstanding. If you will please give us another chance, I promise you there are many sincere people who are trying to learn how to love others better.

When it comes to issues of a sensitive nature, the church tends to shy away from topics they feel ill equipped to address. Sometimes that means they also distance themselves from those who have issues that make them feel awkward or uncomfortable. That's where we all need personal growth and to work on love and acceptance. The subject in this book deals with things that people don't often want to address because it makes them feel uncomfortable. Pornography, lust, and demonic torment from sexual demons are not exactly casual dinner conversation. You're probably not going to hear it preached on a Sunday morning, either. For the most part, the unspoken message that is conveyed is, *"We don't talk about that here."*

Many spiritual leaders are overworked and overwhelmed

with the demands set before them. They should be commended for their commitment to a very demanding job. While it is not my intent to convey any negativity towards spiritual leadership, the reality is sometimes pastors and ministry leaders are not always experienced with inner healing and deliverance ministry. Many people, in fact, have such a negative definition in their mind about the word 'deliverance,' that it repels them from learning more. I hope that I can help people rephrase and redefine that definition so that others think of it more as 'compassionate healing and restoration.'

Let's take a deeper look at why there seems to be a void in the body of Christ concerning this area of ministry. First of all, it takes a commitment and a dependence on the Holy Spirit, and a diligence to hear from God. Not all pastors and churches believe the gifts of the Spirit are for today. Some come from a theological background that has taught them that everything was finished with the apostles and prophets in biblical times, and they believe the gifts of the Spirit are not for today. They may believe that God only speaks through the scriptures and that prophetic gifts no longer exist. That, however, is an erroneous view, proven by the many people that do operate in the gifts of the Spirit. If they were not for today, they would not be available to anyone.

There is another perspective on deliverance where people tend to think demons are everywhere and responsible for every problem. That, too, is an unbalanced point of view. Depending on what theological school of thought people come from determines a person's perspective. I once talked to a pastor's wife that was so fearful of the term 'deliverance' because it conjured up this image in her mind of people throwing up frogs in a bucket. I laughed and tried to reassure her that Holy Spirit is a gentleman, and He is not there as some strange circus act. I've been delivered from an awful lot but I've never done that! That negative impression obviously got lodged in her mind from somewhere, but that strange thought was tied to fear that the Holy Spirit would do something to embarrass her and cause confusion in the church. Instead of trusting the Holy Spirit, she feared and distrusted Him. Needless to say, the fear in the leadership caused the church to take on a form of church, but without any power or effectiveness.

People are trained to deal with spiritual issues in different ways. Not all of them are profitable. For instance, some ministry leaders view addictions and other problems as more of a mental health issue rather than an inner healing or a deliverance issue. If a leader feels that something is beyond their area of expertise, they may cease looking for spiritual answers and refer those individuals to professional counselors, rehabs or outpatient services. All addictions are rooted in a need to feel loved, valued and respected. The spirits connected to them are fear, rejection, abandonment and unloving spirits; but sexual addictions also include spirits of lust, covetousness, the perverse spirit, idolatry, and usually, witchcraft. Sometimes spirits stemming from rape, incest, molestation and soul ties can also be a part of the issue. It's not that the role of mental health professionals are not valued or needed, but the approach to addressing certain spiritual issues can be vastly different and get much different results. Natural solutions are insufficient for spiritual issues. **Demons do not respond to counseling. They respond to the authority of Christ.**

Still another perspective is that people may feel that this ministry of rescue and liberation falls under the category of someone that is uniquely gifted for this type of ministry. If pastors do not feel they have that type of person in their congregation, they may look to other ministries outside of their local church to provide that type of service. Others subscribe to the school of thought that says that what is needed is to 'put off the flesh' and the root of the problem lies in a lack of discipline. They believe more doctrine is necessary in order to crucify the flesh. While there is a degree of truth in this line of thinking, it's not all about discipline. I tried desperately to be disciplined, yet I remained bound to the enemy because I couldn't determine what was keeping the door open. I needed mature, compassionate, prophetic ministry. This sort of belief becomes legalism and condemnation to those who are struggling with demonic oppression because they can never measure up. This is the warning the Apostle Paul left us in the Book of Galatians, not to come under 'bewitchment' and the deception of legalistic doctrine.

There is a lot of conflicting information out there, some declaring that casting out demons, inner healing and tearing down spiritual strongholds are not biblical. Some say that freeing people from demonic oppression is not a ministry function or mandate. Others may claim that God has not revealed the names of certain spirits over cities, nations or other strongmen in His word, and that those are secrets that are not known to man. They fear the information must be revealed by demons from the underworld. Even more declare that we need not give much thought to the enemy because he is defeated by the power of the cross. These are limited perspectives that make allowances for things people either don't understand or things for which they don't have answers. There are multiple scriptures to refute the misconceptions from those that don't have the confidence in knowing how to help set the captives free. Jesus demonstrated by example the works that we are called to:

"And these signs will accompany those who believe: In my name they will drive out demons; they will speak in new tongues..." (Mark 16:17 NIV)

"Heal the sick, raise the dead, cleanse those who have leprosy, drive out demons. Freely you have received; freely give." (Matthew 10:8 NIV)

That is a clear mandate to do the works that Jesus did. In regards to secret knowledge, no one should be relying on information from an ungodly source, but God has said in his word,

"For the Lord GOD does nothing without revealing his secret to his servants the prophets." (Amos 3:7 NIV)

"No longer do I call you servants, for a servant does not understand what his master is doing. But I have called you friends, because everything I have learned from My Father I have made known to you." (John 15:15 NIV)

"The king answered Daniel and said, "Surely your God is a God of gods and a Lord of kings and a revealer of mysteries, since you have been able to reveal this mystery." (Daniel 2:47 NIV)

"Hear now My words: If there is a prophet among you, I, the LORD, make Myself known to him in a vision; I speak to him in a dream" (Numbers 12:6, NKJV)

So you see, God does reveal secrets and mysteries all the time. There is a huge difference between teaching the word of God and sharing what comes as revelation. **Ministry that liberates others from the shackles of bondage is not always connected to doctrine. It is connected to the revelation of what is taking place in a particular person's life, and revealing what opened the door to demonic oppression, torment, illness and other curses. Inner healing and deliverance is directly connected to healing lies in people's belief systems.** It is impossible to help someone get delivered in our own strength. As a matter of fact, it is impossible to do any real work of the ministry through our own strength. All authentic ministry must come from the Holy Spirit. That is why the gifts of the Spirit are such a vital part of any life-giving ministry. We are dependent upon Holy Spirit to reveal the secrets and mysteries that are beyond our knowledge.

Rescuing people from the bondages of evil is a vital part of the Christian life. People often require assistance in getting free. Not all understand where the enemy secured an open door and they need to be counseled by the Holy Spirit. But, with that said, let me make an important point. People that are held captive by the devil have one choice, and only one choice: obey the word of God, or remain stuck. There really is no other option. God is compassionate towards us, but He is never soft on sin.

The other reality is, there are many people who are in ministry and demons have them in chains, but they're not talking about it. They're afraid to talk about it because they're afraid of losing ministry, reputation, friends and perhaps even their marriage. Their spouses are just as trapped, forced to keep up the charade. They feel hurt because they've lost respect for someone they used to hold in high regard, and they can't stand feeling that they're living one way in public and another reality in private. We are supposed to be doing the works that Jesus did – healing the sick, raising the dead, and casting out demons. Instead, it's like the body of Christ is being held hostage by the enemy. The body of Christ has been weak, sick and diseased by spiritual parasites. No one should tolerate the enemy covering them with reproach. These issues must be addressed so that people can get the help they need!

When people are hindered in asking for help, they find themselves in prison. They become bound in every way possible, afraid that someone will discover their secret sin. And so, isolated by their own fear of discovery and embarrassment, they remain bound to shame, fear, and insecurity. The fear of losing face in front of others is very real. The fear of admitting personal failure, addiction or bondage is sometimes so painful and embarrassing that people cannot bring themselves to be honest with others about the issues of their life. It could be about a lot of things. People tend to want to avoid pain, but in our inability to face our own sin, our lack of trust towards the Lord and others places us in the enemy's hands. This is why people often remain stuck in the very sin that they despise. It breaks God's heart to see His children enslaved, and He wants to deliver them from the fear of asking for help. As we can see in the following verse, God's desire is for our restoration. Because we can be confident in His desire to restore us, we can also be confident that He knows exactly *who* can help us and *how* to help us in our time of need. What a great comfort!

"But this is a people plundered and looted; they are all of them trapped in holes and hidden in prisons; they have become plunder with none to rescue, spoil with none to say, "Restore!" (Isaiah 42:22, English Standard Version).

Condemnation and guilt can be suffocating. The more a

person is bound by sin and shame, the more they will live by false pretense. They will try to put on an outward appearance that everything is ok, but this results in a person that lives in a constant performance mentality. It will eventually choke the life out of anyone that falls into that trap.

"Fear of man will prove to be a snare, but whoever trusts in the LORD is kept safe." (Proverbs 29:25)

I read somewhere that a large church took an anonymous survey of those that were plagued by spirits of lust, incubus and succubus. One statistic had it as high as 7 out of 10 people that struggle with this issue, yet no one seems to be talking about it. **7 out of 10!** Although I could not find the exact source of that information, I did find another source of information that is equally disappointing, but it shows just how real the struggle is for a lot of people. In a 2014 survey of church leaders, 50 percent of pastors and 68 percent of Christian men confessed they visit some source of online porn weekly.[5] If you are one of those statistics, you're definitely not alone. Can you imagine the amount of unclean spirits attached to people's lives that keep

---

[5] Wiles, J., Porn Epidemic in Churches Prompts Christian Filmmakers to Rally Pastors, June 11, 2014, Christian Newswire.

them locked behind walls of shame, fear of judgment and rejection? How can people get delivered if no one talks about it?

I grew up in the presence of demonic spirits that were with me all my life. I did not know where the door came open, they just always seemed to be there. I remember being a very young child and sensing unusual things in my life. Even as a little child, I knew there were things within my own family life that were dysfunctional. Whether from extreme poverty, where we lived, or my dad's mental illness issues, it just felt like we had all been cloaked in shame and rejection. It was always there. I realize now it was the stain of generations of sin, but I didn't understand that then. I just always felt this sense of rejection and being an outcast. There was also a sense of being watched, like there was some invisible presence around me. They were familiar spirits but I did not know that then, either. Fear and insecurity were huge in my life. I also had an unnatural attraction to the supernatural and occult. Lust had been with me since I was a child. I remember having thoughts and feelings that were very inappropriate at such a young age. Even by the age of 5 or 6, I knew there was something unclean about the thoughts and feelings I experienced. When a person has demonic spirits attached to their life, those spirits will always look for a place to manifest.

Sometime in my early teens I saw a horror movie on TV that involved a paranormal spirit raping a woman in her sleep. I was struck with both fear and fascination, and it seemed to be a door the enemy used to gain even more access to my life. It wasn't long after seeing that movie that I began to have demonic nighttime visitations. I could tell that a spirit was touching me without my permission. I never saw a form but I knew when it was there. The demonic presence brought fear, but the sensations were pleasurable and arousing, so it quickly became habitual. This became an agreement in the spirit realm that bound me to Lust for many years. It would be at least another twenty years before I got saved, and even more than that before I was able to finally get free.

Never think, "Oh, it's just a movie. It isn't real. There's no harm in in." Not everything comes without injury to your spirit, mind and emotions. The enemy knows if he can seduce your mind then eventually you will give him your body. Guard yourself and your children from watching certain things because the enemy is always looking for a way in. As a teen and young adult, I was extremely lonely and depressed. I tried desperately to fill the gaping hole in my heart. I longed for love but looked for it in all the wrong places. The more I participated in sin, the more I felt depressed, rejected, unclean and guilty. It became a horrible negative cycle of seeking validation and comfort, only to feel more guilt, condemnation and shame. In my teenage mind, sex equated to love. What I really desired was love, acceptance and comfort from the deep sense of loneliness and rejection.

We are made for intimacy. It's a longing to be known, loved and accepted, but far too often people look for those needs to be filled in an illegitimate way. When we try to fulfill legitimate needs in an illegitimate manner, the result is condemnation, feelings of guilt and shame. The void is designed by God to be fulfilled through Him. Pouring out our heart in praise and worship help fill that desire to feel loved and accepted. It also allows us to know Him, because He often communicates His thoughts towards us as we enter into worship. This is the answer to our need for intimacy.

Generational curses and demonic attachments existed in my family before I was born, which contributed to my brokenness. I also opened doors to the enemy through my own sin. I lived in bondage for many years and became a magnet for others with demons attached to their lives. Every time a person has sex outside of marriage they are committing sin. We know this through scripture. (1 Cor.6:13 - 19; Rom. 13:9; Acts 15:20). God's plan for sex is through the covenant of marriage. Many people in this day and age do not wait for marriage. Through the act of intimacy, they form soul ties with others. They go from one sexual partner to another, dishonoring themselves in the process, leaving pieces of themselves behind. This leaves people with wounds of rejection, shame and guilt, which causes their souls to become fragmented and scattered. It also produces demonic attachments. Every demon that was active in the life of a previous sexual partner, and all their partners before them, can then become attached to the person they slept with. It's like spiritual venereal disease. Lust and other spirits can be transferred through physical contact much like a disease is spread through germs. Many people do not realize that demons in one person's life will strategize with demons in other people's lives in order to continue to reproduce cycles of brokenness, bondage, pain and suffering. Darkness attracts more darkness, and unclean spirits are attracted to one another. Satan was my master and as such, he overpowered me. When a person is under the dominion of another master, they are subject to the will of that master.

When I got saved, those spirits didn't automatically leave. Though I tried very hard to fill my life with good, godly things and I was very committed to serving God, nothing severed the demonic attachments. I continued to feel an unclean, ungodly presence molesting me at night and in my dreams. I prayed and sought God for help, seemingly to no avail. I wanted to be set free, but I was too ashamed to approach anyone with my problem. I felt there was no one to turn to; no one that I felt would understand or know how to help me. It's a horrible place to be, and many people are stuck in that very place right now.

The church made it seem as if willpower was the key to living free. Just stay in the word and live right. That was a religious answer, but not a spiritual one. While abstaining from certain activities can certainly help a person *stay* free, that is not the answer to *getting* free. That is such a simple and inadequate answer to a very complex issue. That was not all there was to it. I needed deliverance, but the people in my life at the time did not have the answers because the church barely mentioned deliverance, if at all. The fear of rejection and being judged by others in the church was too great. I remember one particular woman there who did have the gift of discerning of spirits, but she was also terribly immature in that gift and had a critical attitude. One day as we were talking, she abruptly looked at me with disgust, rolled her eyes and said, "Ugh, there is such a spirit of lust on you! You need to do something about that!" And she walked away. I was shocked, hurt and humiliated. I felt like telling her, "Congratulations. You succeeded in humiliating another human being. Well done." All it did was reinforce my sense of shame and the inability to have a sense of confidence towards trusting others in the church. I felt so unclean and ashamed to admit the nature of the problem. I could not bring myself to ask about such an uncomfortable subject. I believe many people have also met with the same judgmental attitudes of others in the church. Sometimes even pastors and other ministers fail to exhibit the compassion that is needed to truly help others navigate their path to freedom. It's ok to admit when that is not your level of expertise, but I believe the church has a responsibility to provide *someone* knowledgeable and anointed that can help. People are hurting and they need help. My hope in being transparent on this subject is to help others understand the incredible amount of courage it takes for people to ask for help when they are covered in deep shame. We cannot afford to turn anyone away without the answers and help that they need.

I finally got saved when I was 32, but I was not free. The man that later became my husband had some frustrations of his own he was trying to work through. He, too, felt bound by fear. He felt there was no one he could trust to confide his struggles. He was a pastor at the time he faced his struggles, but felt very alone in the battle. The thought of how to address his personal life issues was incredibly intimidating. Ministers fear rejection and judgment from their peers just like anyone else and probably more so, because they are standing in front of others as an example. When people look to you as a role model, admitting that you are struggling with demonic strongholds is quite difficult. Fear of disgrace keeps many people silent when they should be able to reach out to someone for help. It doesn't even have to be lust, pornography or a sexual issue; it could be anger or some other sin that people have a difficult time admitting. When Satan is allowed to silence people then they can never get the help that is needed.

It is so important to find someone that has both the knowledge and experience that can help with the issue at hand, as well as someone that can be trusted to keep a confidence. People will not ask for help if they do not trust others to honor things said in confidence. The enemy is well aware how to wield the weapon of shame. You can't heal what someone is hiding. Pride often masquerades as fear. It keeps people locked up behind walls of performance and pretense. Pride is simply an artificial shell that tries to protect us from the feeling of fear. Fear often comes from shame or the feeling that others will betray us. Feelings that we don't know how to resolve are difficult, but it takes baby steps to trust others. Take a step of faith. Instead of feeling paralyzed by fear and shame, ask God who you can trust with your problem. Trust Him to lead you to the right person. We all have to face our Goliaths, but God will help you take the enemy down.

Father,

I thank You that You know my struggles. You know everything about me, and You are well acquainted with everything the enemy has done to bind me with guilt, condemnation and shame. I thank You for loving me unconditionally and accepting me just as I am. I am accepted in Christ. Help me to develop intimacy with You so that I can learn how to delight myself in You. I also thank You for leading me into truth and understanding that will make me free. I yield my thoughts to You now so that You can show me the path to freedom. In Jesus name, amen.

CHAPTER 2
EVIL INHERITANCES

An inheritance is something that is received from a predecessor; usually a deceased family member. It can be money, property or some other material possession. People also inherit genealogical traits such as the color of their hair, eyes, or the shape of their facial features. Spiritually speaking, a person can inherit both good and bad things. A good inheritance would be related to the person's calling, destiny or spiritual gifting. Often it is evident that spiritual gifting such as a prophetic or teaching mantle remains in certain families as a blessed inheritance from God. An evil inheritance, however, is something that is received as a result of a curse. It is passed from one person to another in a family through parents, grandparents and other ancestors. When people fail to ask forgiveness for their sins and those sins do not have the blood of Jesus to cleanse them away, then the sin weaknesses and the familiar spirits that are assigned to keep people in bondage remain in a family, to be passed on as an evil inheritance. The unsuspecting recipient is then left to deal with the trouble caused by those demonic spirits.

I would think that no parent would want to leave that sort of an inheritance for their children. Unfortunately, some do simply because they convince themselves that there is no need to deal with those spiritual matters. There can be many things that the spirit realm is quite aware of that we are not, and it's the things that we are blind to that become the doors the enemy uses to gain access to our lives. That is why it becomes so important to teach on the necessity of being *intentional*, thereby taking deliberate action to cleanse our families from bloodline curses. Give yourself and your family the opportunity to have a better future! There is a prayer to renounce generational curses in the final chapter.

Miriam Webster Dictionary defines a curse as: 1) a prayer or invocation for harm or injury to come upon someone; 2) something that is cursed or accursed; 3) evil or misfortune that comes as if in response to imprecation or as retribution; and 4) a cause of great harm or misfortune: also torment.

The first illustration refers to various forms of witchcraft, such as hexes, incantations and word curses, but let me also share an example of how Christians can unknowingly cross a line into these things and operate in the same spirit.

When I first got saved, I knew nothing at all about prayer. I hadn't been raised in church so I had no point of reference. Therefore, the way I learned was by listening to how others in my ladies home group prayed. I looked up to a couple of the women there and tried to learn from them. The problem was some of their prayers were more of a curse than a blessing. Sometimes they would pray things like, "God, shake them over hell but don't let them fall in. Teach them a lesson that they won't forget. Get them to stop messing around with sin. Bring them into the kingdom." There was a tendency to pray out of judgement and frustration with people's sin rather than being motivated by love. They also prayed that God would expose people's sin and basically shame them into repentance. I didn't realize for a long time that this type of prayer was essentially asking God to clothe people in condemnation and curse them. Unfortunately, I took many of my cues from them simply because I didn't know any different. People are under enough condemnation. If people are disobedient to God, then the curse is already at work in their lives. We don't need to pray for them to receive more problems. Jesus came to remove our condemnation! Praying soulish prayers crosses a line into witchcraft. It is the attempt to bring to pass the will of an individual rather than

God, and it opens a door for the curse to come back on the person that does so, especially if that person is already a Christian.[6] Jesus advised us to bless and not curse, and to speak blessing over others.[7] He advised us not to retaliate or take vengeance into our own hands. His word counsels us to speak life and not death. These are important things to remember. If you have opened a door to witchcraft and rebellion in some of the things you have said towards others, then repent and ask God to break the power of those negative words so that you are not operating in a spirit of witchcraft and inviting a curse to come back on you.

The second point made by Webster's dictionary is something that is cursed or accursed. Some people seem to have more than their fair share of problems. Whether it's related to health problems, things constantly breaking down or problems that keep draining a person's finances, those things can be directly related to cursed items or other unbroken curses. God gave us a warning about these sort of things to let us know that yes, they do exist, and people will suffer the consequences if they take these things into their homes.

---

[6] Genesis 12:3; Ps. 109:17-18

[7] Romans 12:14, Luke 6:28, Matt. 5:43

"Neither shalt though bring an abomination into thine house, lest though be a cursed thing like it: but thou shalt utterly detest it, for it is a cursed thing" (Deut. 7:26 KJV)

Cursed objects are things such as statues of gods and cultic objects of various religions, other artwork depicting false gods or idols, amulets, lucky charms and things associated with fortunes, letters that have curse words in them, tarot cards, Ouija boards, prayer candles, crystals used in energy healing, obelisks and other things used specifically in occult magic. There is a curse attached to them. This thought is supported by scripture.[8] Anything that is an idol or something that others worship in a different religion is specifically forbidden by God. Buddha is one very popular idol, as is the Catholic statue of Mary. Other 'saints,' gods or goddesses, and décor items from other nations can also carry a curse.

Sometimes inanimate objects can have a curse put on them for specific purposes. People can actually buy cursed objects online so that they can be given away to unsuspecting individuals, and they end up taking that object into their home. It's true. I've spoken with people that have admitted they or their family were involved in many of those

---

[8] Deut. 7:25,26; Is. 47: 11-14

practices before they got saved. Those from Africa, Native American and Spanish origins are peculiarly prone to having witchcraft in their ancestry. Some of those objects are cursed with a curse that compels people to hold on to them, even though they have been warned and made aware there is a curse on them! They refuse to believe that the thing is harmful. That is how the enemy puts a curse of deception on things, so that people keep cursed objects in their possession. Even though the person that has a cursed object may not be praying to it or using it in a manner consistent with occult magic, it can still have a curse attached to it if someone else put it there. That is why we should never argue with something that is even slightly in question. If something doesn't feel right about a particular thing, just get it out of the house and pray to break the power of any evil powers associated with it. Better to be safe than sorry and live with a curse. Part of living in relationship with God is to correct ourselves when we come to realize that something in our life is not pleasing to Him.

The third and fourth points in Webster's definition deal with the effects of a curse. A curse produce many things. It produces loss, defeat, failure, and an inability to prosper. The spirits of death and hell are attached to everything in that person's life. It causes health issues, mental and emotional troubles, hopelessness, fear, loss of finances, unstable or loss of employment, instability, broken relationships, divorce and many other troubles. Sometime it feels like your wallet has holes in it. Things just keep happening to drain your account. Nothing works right and it's impossible to get ahead. A wounded person that is in bondage cannot successfully fulfill their destiny. There is a sense of spiritual weakness, frustration and loss that comes from all the heaviness. Loss produces shame, insecurity, inferiority and a sense of condemnation.

Blessings, however, cause a person to do well and prosper. As a person's soul prospers, other aspects of their life are healed and they are empowered to fulfill their calling. This also fills a person's life with a sense of fulfillment and purpose, which releases joy and strength. It's the complete opposite effect. When the blessings flow, the person's restoration is released. If only a limited amount of blessings occur, then there can be something blocking that individual's progress.

I took the time to explain how these things can affect a person's life because many times people don't know they need to take those things into consideration. Getting free from demonic oppression is not just a simple answer like, "Just don't do that anymore." Unfortunate as it is, **spirits of lust and other sexual demons can be received as an evil**

inheritance and a generational curse, which means that those spirits have created strongholds in the believer's life since the time they were born. These spirits are so insidious in the way they worm their way deep in the mind of their victim. It is incredibly difficult to recognize these spirits when a person has made alliances with them. The lies, the way the person's world view, self-image and belief system have all been shaped has been influenced by the enemy. Even a person's sexual preferences can be influenced by the familiar spirits of whatever they've been born into. They can't distinguish between what is truly them and what comes from an evil influence. That is why people can genuinely say, "I was born this way. It's just who I am," and believe it, because they sincerely believe there can be no other explanation. Sometimes the thoughts and beliefs in a person's mind will create such a crookedness in them that it causes them to sin against others in some very bad ways. While it never excuses wrong behavior, knowing how the enemy works against people to create a false identity in them does make it easier to understand. People will defend their allegiance towards these spirits because they become convinced that particular behaviors, personal preferences and habits are a part of their identity. The enemy has claimed their thought life as his turf, and only the Holy Spirit can reach them to show them the lie.

Lust, bitterness, idolatry and witchcraft are all very strong, stubborn spirits that work together. Depending on how long they have been in a person's life or if they have been in a family for generations can have a lot to do with the level of difficulty in the person receiving deliverance. Some spirits are more stubborn than others. They can have a very complex and tangled root system. It is very important that the person cooperates with God in self-deliverance so that they understand how to maintain their freedom once they are set free.

The first thing people need to understand is that whether it concerns incubus/succubus demons, addictions or any other demonic spirit that is attached to their life, the process of getting free is going to require work on the part of the individual. Many people just want to be free from the demonic spirits that are tormenting them, but not everyone wants to live as a Christian. Freedom never comes without personal responsibility. We must own our sin. We must own the sin of our ancestors, whether we participated in it or not. If it's in our generational line, it's ours by inheritance.

While a Christian can exercise their authority in Christ and command a demon to leave another person, we have to consider that may not always be the best solution. For one thing, demons don't always have to go. If the individual has formed some sort of agreement with them and does not genuinely repent, the demon knows it has a legal right to be there. Another example would be if the person is holding on to a grudge or unforgiveness towards someone else. Anger comes from a sense of injustice and must be dealt with in a scriptural and spiritual manner in order to resolve it at the root. Unless the person works through the issue to the point of genuine forgiveness, this grants the demon a legal right to remain in the person's life due to their sin and disobedience. (Unforgiveness is a very common door that people may not connect to issues with sexual demons). It can be irresponsible to cast out a spirit if the individual is not willing to take personal responsibility for their sin, because those spirits will just come back even stronger. A demon will come back into a house that hasn't been swept clean and filled with the Holy Spirit. (See Matthew 12:43,33 & Luke 11:24,25).

It is very important to fill that void with good and godly things that fill up the space so that there isn't room for demons to come back. Prayer, worship, the infilling of the Holy Spirit, reading the word of God, speaking in tongues and healthy relationships that provide a sense of love and accountability are vital to spiritual health and personal growth. It's like hanging the "NO VACANCY" sign and letting bad spirits know there's no more room for them!

Deep cleansing prayers that involve renouncing the sins of the past and that of our ancestors can be helpful in breaking down strongholds and sending evil spirits back to the pit of hell where they belong.

CHAPTER 3
INCUBUS AND SUCCUBUS – WHAT ARE THEY?

I understand that this is a topic that's probably controversial depending on who you're talking to, but as one who had years of first-hand experience with these things, I can tell you without a shadow of a doubt; it's not all folklore, myths and made up stories. Incubus and succubus spirits are real.

First of all, what are they? An incubus or succubus spirit is a demonic spirit that will come and lie upon someone in order to have sex with a person. It usually occurs at night, but I had it happen when I was awake, too. I could feel something touching me in a very real way, and it wasn't my imagination. A demonic presence was involved.

"An incubus (nominal form constructed from the Latin verb, incubo, incubare, or "to lie upon") is a Lilin demon in male form who, according to a number of mythological and legendary traditions, lies upon sleepers, especially women, in order to have sexual intercourse with them. Its female counterpart is the succubus." [9] "The word incubus is derived from late Latin incubo (a nightmare induced by such a demon); from incub(āre) (to lie upon)." [10] "It is said that Lilu disturbs and seduces women in their sleep, while Lilitu, a female demon, appears to men in their erotic dreams." [11] The Jewish Encyclopedia notes that there are three demons called Lilu, Lilit, and Ardat Lilit with the second being referenced in Isaiah 34:14. [12]

"The desert creatures will meet with the wolves, The hairy goat also will cry to its kind; Yes, the night monster will settle there and will find herself a resting place." (New American Standard)

According to the Jewish Encyclopedia online, there are three classes of demons that are mentioned: spirits, devils and lilin. "The first have neither body nor form; the second

[9] Stephens, Walter (2002), Demon Lovers, p. 23, The University of Chicago Press, ISBN 0-226-77261-6; as noted on Wikepedia under "Incubus."

[10] "Incubus". Reference.com. Retrieved September 26, 2014.

[11] Raphael Patai, p. 221, The Hebrew Goddess: Third Enlarged Edition, ISBN 978-0-8143-2271-0

[12] "Incubus" . By Emil G. Hirsch, Solomon Schechter, Ludwig Blau, retrieved January 9, 2017, The Jewish Encyclopedia.

appear in complete human shape; the third in human shape, but with wings." One woman that I counseled confided that she awoke one night to a very large demon in her bed. She said what woke her up was the fact that she kicked a foot in her sleep, but she was not married and there was not supposed to be anyone else in her bed. She was sleeping alone – or so she thought. This woman described this demon to be around 8-9 feet tall and said it was the most terrifying thing that had ever happened to her. A different person, a young man, described some sort of a demon that was in his room that came and jumped on him and had sex with him. Do I still have questions about this sort of thing? Sure. These are odd stories but I believe the Lord allowed these people to see, feel and experience the evil that had been invited in to their lives. They are obviously tormented by these experiences and they are asking for help. I know that the thought of this type of encounter may raise questions or objections in the minds of some people because they may have a hard time believing it to be true, but these are just a couple of examples of people that have described situations where they saw demons in some physical form. There are too many unrelated people describing these similarities to simply ignore.

Scripture does tell us that demons go out looking for people to inhabit because they are looking for a place of embodiment. However there are other scriptures that also say that demons can assume a form that is *other than human*.[13] Please be careful not to discount other people's experiences just because you may not have experienced it or it doesn't fit with your theology. Some people can see these things while others don't, but just because one person can't see what someone else has, doesn't mean it doesn't exist. The spirit realm is very real; we just can't always see what is going on there unless God allows it. Demons are tormenting people and they need help for their distress.

I can also confirm that some of these spirits do take a more human form. Some years ago, the Lord gave me an incredibly clear dream. It was more of a night vision, actually. I felt like I was awake and standing there in front of it. The demon I saw was in vivid detail. I saw a beautiful blonde female demon dressed in a sexy black lace dress. She had huge black wings, and she hung in mid-air right in front of our bedroom window. As she looked down upon our bed, instantly I knew her assignment. She was there as a succubus spirit sent to tempt my husband. I sat up in bed and out of a sound sleep I yelled, "Who are you, O dark witch of the night? Get out!"

---

[13] 2 Cor. 11:14,15; Rev. 13:1-18; Rev. 9:2,3; Rev. 16:13

The next day I spoke with my husband and shared what I had seen. He thanked me and remarked that he had felt the enemy trying to get at him, but once I shared the vision of the demonic temptress, he immediately felt strength from the Holy Spirit rise up inside of him. He took authority over those thoughts so that the enemy could not find an open door. Praise God for the victory! Holy Spirit wants to be an integral part of helping to protect our marriage and families. He wants to expose the assignments of the enemy so that Satan doesn't get a foothold in our relationships, but it starts with us. Sit down with your spouse and invite Holy Spirit into your marriage. Make a covenant between the three of you, giving Holy Spirit the right to step in and help you. It is so important to realize that many of the thoughts and feelings we have are a set up by the enemy in order to get us to make an agreement with him in the spirit realm. When we do, then he has been granted access. It's like giving him the keys to the house. Lying spirits and seducing spirits will whisper in a person's ears to try to get them to justify wrong behaviors.

Ancient Jewish superstitions depict Lilith as a nocturnal demon that took the shape of a night owl that went around stealing children. Arabic translators render the word in Isaiah 34:14 by "ghul," which is identical with the "lamia" of the

Vulgate. [14] In ancient Greek mythology, Lamia was a beautiful queen of Libya who became a child-eating demon.[15] She also has a serpent's tail or snakeskin wrapped around her arm and waist. This spirit is associated with hypocrisy, jealousy, envy, prophecy or divination, spiritual blindness, miscarriage and reproductive problems. Notice that all those things are indicative of the religious spirit of legalism, which is another manifestation of witchcraft. The characteristics of this spirit are interchangeable with sorcery. Later traditions referred to many *lamiae*; these were folkloric monsters similar to vampires and succubae that seduced young men and then fed on their blood.[16] Lilith, or perhaps Lamia, as this spirit is referred to in Arabic, is reportedly responsible for causing miscarriages and infant death. These spirits (Lamia & lamiae, incubus, succubus by the names of Lilin, Lilith, Lilu) really do act as vampire spirits. Some individuals have even reported to have felt as if their soul is being sucked out of them, like wind rushing out of their nose and mouth. The person is left feeling drained of energy.

---

[14] "Incubus". By Emil G. Hirsch, Solomon Schechter, Ludwig Blau, retrieved January 9, 2017, The Jewish Encyclopedia.

[15] Jøn, A. Asbjørn (2003). "Vampire Evolution". Metaphor. English Teachers Association of NSW (August): 19–23.

[16] Information on Lamia from the Online Encyclopedia.

Lilith is known by many other names in various languages and countries throughout the world. These stories have been around for thousands of years and the Bible does give reference to them. Lilith is mentioned as a screech owl spirit, an unclean spirit that brings fear and terror by night in Isaiah 34:14-15.

"And desert creatures will meet with hyenas, and goat-demons will call out to each other. There also Liliths will settle, and find for themselves a resting place. Owls will nest there, lay eggs, hatch them, and care for their young under the shadow of their wings; yes indeed, vultures will gather there, each one with its mate." (Isaiah 34:14-15 ISV)

Variations of scripture sometimes state the word Lilith in place of the screech owl. Others refer to the arrow snake, night monsters, hairy creatures and goat demons. In the Dead Sea Scrolls' Songs of the Sage the term first occurs in a list of monsters. In Jewish magical inscriptions on bowls and amulets from the 6th century CE onwards, Lilith is identified as a female demon and the first visual depictions appear.[17] The interesting thing about Lilith is that it is

---

[17] Kristen E. Kvam, Linda S. Schearing, Valarie H. Ziegler Eve and Adam: Jewish, Christian, and Muslim readings on Genesis and gender Bloomington: Indiana University Press, 1999. p174 "Other scholars, such as Lowell K. Handy, agree

mentioned in the Hebrew texts, Greek, Latin and many other languages. It also appears in the Talmud, the Kabbalah and in the occult writings of Aleister Crowley. Two organizations that use initiations and magic associated with Lilith are the *Ordo Antichristianus Illuminati* and the *Order of Phosphorus*. Lilith appears as a succubus in Aleister Crowley's *De Arte Magica*. Many early occult writers that contributed to modern day Wicca expressed special reverence for Lilith.[18] Some authors feel that this is the 'strange woman,' or seductress referred to in Proverbs 2,5,7,9.

This spirit that brings fear and terror at night can also bring feelings of sexual pleasure, which can cause very conflicting feelings in the individual. There can be a great deal of guilt over enjoying something that a person knows is wrong, yet the pleasure part is what the enemy counts on so that people will keep the door open to him. There are many references in the Bible to spirits that will tempt, seduce, entice and lure people into sin.

These spirits, also known as a mare or goblin spirit in

---

that Lilith is derived from Mesopotamian demons but argue against finding evidence of the Hebrew Lilith in many of the epigraphical and artifactual sources frequently cited as such (e.g., the Sumerian Gilgamesh fragment, the Sumerian incantation from Arshlan-Tash)."

[18] Grimassl, Raven.Stregheria: La Vecchia Religione.

other nationalities, have the ability to make a person feel like a heavy weight is sitting on their chest. They may make their victim feel paralyzed and unable to move or speak. They touch a person sexually and have the ability to rape and have sex with individuals. Succubae and Incubi are the same demonic entity only to be described differently based on the sexes being conversed with.[19] In other words, the same spirit changes into either male or female form depending on the person they are visiting. They are also reportedly bi-sexual. Let me address one question that is sure to arise. Some people would say that spirits are genderless and therefore cannot be male or female. While that is true, we also know that scripture tells us that Satan 'masquerades' as an angel of light. Meaning, he has supernatural ability to disguise himself as he chooses. We know that he appeared in the form of the serpent in the garden when he appeared for the purpose of tempting Eve into sin. It stands to reason that some demons can take different forms based on their personality, character and assignment. The enemy knows how to tailor his bait to the desires of his prey. Scripture also tells us to 'test the spirits,' in 1 John 4:1. There are various kinds of demons each with an assignment to carry out against mankind.

---

[19] Warren, Brett (2016). The Annotated Dæmonologie of King James. A Critical Edition. In Modern English. pp. 79–83. ISBN 1-5329-6891-4.

Incubus and Succubus are reported to affect child-bearing, fertility, miscarriage and more. These demonic spirits can reportedly cause childhood trauma, abuse, and infant death. They can also cause untold marital and relationship problems.

In some nations, especially in African culture, incubus and succubus are known as spirit wives or spirit husbands. **In the spirit realm it is a marriage**, that is why getting free requires cutting those spirits off completely. They must be divorced through prayers of renouncement as well as a firm commitment to living a sanctified life. These spirits are very jealous for the individual for which they are connected. They will cause relationship splits both in couples that are dating, as well as pit spouses against one another in an attempt to cause strife, rejection within the marriage and all kinds of other problems. Their intent is to break up marriages and families. They will also attach themselves to children and attempt to reproduce the same perverse behaviors in the next generation.

Incubus, Succubus and the Kundalini Spirit

Incubus and Succubus are also very connected to the Kundalini spirit. The reason I know that is from the counseling I do with others. I would repeatedly get people complaining of the same type of symptoms. Then one day as I was praying, I started to Google the symptoms. Instantly it came up as the Kundalini spirit! When I inquire into people's past, we can often uncover something in their history that reveals the link to this particular spirit. I have learned to inquire now about people that may have opened a door to the enemy through any sort of New Age practices that refer to 'energy,' 'enlightenment' or even some alternative forms of healing. Acupuncture and Ayurveda are a couple forms of alternative medical practices that can also be a cause. Eastern forms of medicine, healing and religion are intertwined with occult practices. When a person comes by their knowledge through divination and then mixes drugs and other compounds into healing practices, it is called sorcery. These forms of healing and medicines all practice some form of enlightenment and energy healing as well. The source of knowledge comes from calling on false gods and seeking knowledge from an occult source. Then it is passed down to those who teach and train others in the various fields of alternative medicine. Anything that comes as a result of tapping into the occult carries a curse because it is connected to idolatry, and these practices are forbidden by God.

In case you are interested, let me just list some of the

'symptoms' of the Kundalini spirit. The following are either common signs of an awakened Kundalini or symptoms of a problem associated with an awakening Kundalini (commonly referred to as Kundalini syndrome):

- Involuntary jerks, tremors, shaking, itching, tingling, and crawling sensations, especially in the arms and legs (Some describe snakes or crawling sensation traveling in the legs and in the genitals)
- Energy rushes or feelings of electricity circulating the body
- Intense heat (sweating) or cold, especially as energy is experienced passing through the chakras
- Visions or sounds at times associated with a particular chakra
- Diminished or conversely extreme sexual desire sometimes leading to a state of constant or whole-body orgasm
- Emotional upheavals or surfacing of unwanted and repressed feelings or thoughts with certain repressed emotions becoming dominant in the conscious mind for short or long periods of time.[16]
- Headache, migraine, or pressure inside the skull
- Increased blood pressure and irregular heartbeat

- Emotional numbness
- Antisocial tendencies
- Mood swings with periods of depression or mania
- Pains in different areas of the body, especially back and neck
- Sensitivity to light, sound, and touch
- Trance-like and altered states of consciousness
- Disrupted sleep pattern (periods of insomnia or oversleeping)
- Loss of appetite or overeating
- Bliss, feelings of infinite love and universal connectivity, transcendent awareness[20]
- The feeling of having weights around the feet and legs, making walking difficult.

Kundalini can be awakened by spiritual practices such as yoga and meditation. Earlier I quoted the scripture from Isaiah 34:14,15 in regards to Lilith or lilin spirits. The Amplified Bible refers to the arrow snake in verse 15. It is also known as a *coiled* snake. It leaps and jumps on its victim suddenly. Kundalini means 'coiled one' and is considered to be a form of primal energy. It takes the form of a serpent or a goddess and is said to lie at the base of the

---

[20] Shri Mataji Nirmala Devi Srivastava (1997). Meta Modern Era (3rd ed.). Vishwa Nirmala Dharma. pp. 233–248. ISBN 978-8186650059.

spine, waiting to be awakened. It can affect the entire spinal column and even the head. It sits in the lower spine and is said to affect a triangular area, which, coincidentally, is exactly where the sexual organs are located. Different spiritual traditions teach methods of "awakening" kundalini for the purpose of reaching spiritual enlightenment.[21] That is why this spirit is very active in New Age practices. The focus on yoga and many New Age religions is on 'awakening' what are called chakras. Perhaps another way to look at that is entry points into the human soul. As the person releases more and more of themselves to the experience, what they are doing is allowing this spirit to possess their souls with greater degree. Each 'chakra,' I believe, represents an area of the conscious mind that Satan has to overcome in order to convince the person to surrender to his control. The cost is spiritual blindness. The person that has been blinded by the sin of idolatry and has invited some other spirit to take ownership of them eventually loses the power to take back their will. Kundalini has been called an unconscious, instinctive or libidinal force. It is also referred to as 'mother energy' or intelligence of complete maturation".[22]

---

[21] Greer, John Michael (2003). The New Encyclopedia of the Occult (1st ed.). St. Paul, MN: Llewellyn Publications. ISBN 9781567183368.

[22] Sovatsky, Stuart (1998). Words from the Soul: Time, East/West Spirituality, and Psychotherapeutic Narrative. Albany: State University of New York. ISBN 079143950X.

Kundalini awakening is said to result in deep meditation, enlightenment and bliss. It is the same lie that was told to Eve in the garden. If you partake of this, *you will become like God.* New Age philosophies promise that your spirit will be enlightened and free. There's the hook, with the lie attached. If you study more about other people's awakening experiences, they are rarely enjoyable. People have described intense muscle cramps, rigidity and being unable to move for hours at a time, or something within them moving as the war for dominance within their body takes place. Some reports mention feeling their muscles lock up like they were literally folded in half. Others were equally disturbing. I have had people contact me in extreme fear because they can actually feel snakes moving under their skin and they do not know what to do about it. They report uncontrollable orgasms as well as the inability to control arms, legs or other movements. The serpentine spirit takes up residence in the spine, then moves at will within the body. How frightening is that? That is the deception of yoga and other New Age practices. It's like opening Pandora's box. Once it's opened, it can be very difficult indeed to get set free. Participants in yoga and other forms of self-realization practices are encouraged to surrender all they are to the experience: mind, body, soul and spirit. This allows the serpent, or Satan himself, to possess them. It is not coincidental that **witches and wizards are required to do**

the same thing. They must surrender all of themselves to the control of Satan and his demons. The terrible deception of New Age practices such as Kundalini yoga and other religious 'awakening' practices is that those things are essentially turning those people into vessels that the enemy owns. When someone surrenders their will and allows another entity to take over, they have given over their freedom. Satan can then do anything he pleases. They may not understand that is what is happening, but they are willingly surrendering themselves to Satan for his use, and witchcraft will become the primary spirit in their life.

The Kundalini spirit, which also works in tandem with incubus and succubus spirits, lust and witchcraft, also produces sexual pleasure. In order to be set free from the demonic spirits, the individual must repent and renounce these things, even if they seemed to come in as a result of generational curses rather than personal involvement.

Not everyone is a willing participant in yoga or New Age practices, but still have to deal with the effects of curses that have come down their bloodline. Recently I was talking with a couple of individuals that had ancestry from Russia. Their family practiced alternative forms of Eastern medicine. When I asked about a couple of specific things, they admitted that their parents had practiced Ayurveda and other things.

Ayurveda is a system of medicine with historical roots in the Indian subcontinent.[23] Dhanvantari is the Hindu god of Ayurveda. It is an Eastern religion that obtains knowledge through divination. Then it is passed on to others that practice these forms of medicine. Several philosophers in India combined religion and traditional medicine—notable examples being that of Hinduism and Ayurveda.[24]

These practices originate from a false god. **ANY false god is Satan in some form.** It's just that simple. Well known Satanist Aliester Crowley also said to have made use of the Kundalini spirit in his teachings. People don't often realize that certain practices are connected to idolatry and witchcraft spirits, because they are tapping into knowledge that has come from the occult. Any knowledge that is gained from occult powers automatically carries a curse with it because it is a practice forbidden by God.

In Exodus chapter 20, God spoke through Moses to give him the Ten Commandments. God laid out ten directives that would define and shape the lives of His people. Properly understood, all the other teachings, prescriptions, and

---

[23] Meulenbeld, Gerrit Jan (1999). "Introduction". A History of Indian Medical Literature. Groningen: Egbert Forsten. ISBN 9069801248.

[24] Clifford, Terry (2003). Tibetan Buddhist Medicine and Psychiatry. 42. Motilal Banarsidass Publications. ISBN 81-208-1784-2.

directives that come in later chapters derive from these Ten Directives. (VOICE Bible)

"I am the Eternal your God. I led you out of Egypt and liberated you from lives of slavery and oppression." (vs. 2)

"You are not to serve any other gods before Me." (vs.3)

"You are not to make any idol or image of other gods. In fact, you are not to make an image of anything in the heavens above, on the earth below, or in the waters beneath." (vs. 4)

"You are not to bow down and serve any image, for I, the Eternal your God, am a jealous God. As for those who are not loyal to Me, their children will endure the consequences of their sins for three or four generations." (vs.5)

"But for those who love Me and keep My directives, their children will experience My loyal love for a thousand generations." (vs. 6)

"...And do not let your people practice fortune-telling, or use sorcery, or interpret omens, or engage in witchcraft, or cast spells, or function as mediums or psychics, or call forth the spirits of the dead. Anyone who does these things is

detestable to the Lord. It is because the other nations have done these detestable things that the Lord your God will drive them out ahead of you. But you must be blameless before the Lord your God." (Deut. 18:10-13)

'As for the person who turns to mediums and to spiritists, to play the harlot after them, I will also set My face against that person and will cut him off from among his people." (Lev. 20:6)

"But cowards, unbelievers, the corrupt, murderers, the immoral, those who practice witchcraft, idol worshipers, and all liars–their fate is in the fiery lake of burning sulfur. This is the second death." (Rev. 21:8)

Many people have a variety of opinions and ideas because they are unsure about the truth. Please allow me to offer an explanation that I hope will help clarify any misunderstandings. God's word is clear. We cannot afford to compromise with the wrong things for they open us up to demonic oppression. If a person visits a medium or a tarot card reader, for instance, demons have been given legal authority over that person. They also have the legal right to follow that person (and their children) down the bloodline for future generations – UNTIL someone gets saved and renounces those sins. God isn't the only one to keep good records. Demons do too. The penalty for rejecting God *is* severe. Again, it was never God's intention for anyone to end up bearing the same fate as Satan and the fallen angels. He has provided the way of escape through believing in His Son, Jesus Christ, and accepting His invitation to become a child of God. His entire motive for creating mankind was to have sons and daughters who were holy and blameless, *like Him*. He wants relationship with us! If you will continue reading, I will show you the way out of the curse and into a life that is marked by peace, joy and the blessings of God.

"My people are destroyed for lack of knowledge; because you have rejected knowledge, I reject you from being a priest to me. And since you have forgotten the law of your God, I also will forget your children." (Hosea 4:6 ESV)

"Because they have no discipline, their spirits die and their bodies will soon follow; because they are immensely foolish, they wander lost and confused." (Prov. 5:23 VOICE)

The word of God tells us that people are destroyed for lack of knowledge. That is why it is so important not to try to justify our own opinions or erroneous beliefs. In the end, none of that will matter. What will matter is whether or not the blood of Jesus speaks on our behalf and atones for our sins.

So many people are searching for truth, enlightenment, and fulfillment. Their quest for knowledge and understanding has filled them with many confusing thoughts and ideas. The New Age "enlightenment" often appeals to those that are searching because it includes a smorgasbord of ideas and beliefs. It allows an individual to pick and choose from a variety of philosophies that include good works, paths to enlightenment, and spiritual development.

Each person has an inner desire to explore different options and find their way to the truth. We, too, had to go on a journey so that we could make an informed choice what we believe is truth. God gives each person the free will to decide for themselves.

New Age beliefs support many paths to seeking spiritual "light" or enlightenment, which encourages curiosity seekers to find whatever works for them, whether it be meditation, tarot cards, mediums, astrology, spirit guides, or other forms of seeking spiritual revelation. It's not the searching that is wrong, it is going to the wrong source for information. Any information obtained by occult practices is not from God's Holy Spirit. It is from the underworld and it's demons. The problem is the fact that all demons are liars. The truth is not in them. Their sole job description is to kill, steal and destroy, according to scripture. These are Jesus' words as He referred to Satan and his works of darkness.

"The thief comes only to steal and kill and destroy; I have come that they may have life, and have it to the full." (John 10:10)

"...He was a murderer from the beginning. He has always hated the truth, because there is no truth in him. When he lies, it is consistent with his character; for he is a liar and the father of lies." (John 8:44)

New Age beliefs and their practices are not in alignment with truth; therefore they are opposed to the teachings in the Bible. If people are to get free from the things that bind them to curses, there simply cannot be any compromise with deception.

Many people arrive at their judgments by way of their own natural reasoning. However, these are mostly just a variety of opinions. If people insist on navigating their life by their own opinions, then they will always be open to deception. God's word is grounded in truth because a superior being established it. God's word established our entire existence, so it makes sense that He is our source for understanding the spiritual laws by which our world operates.

Jesus sent Holy Spirit to convince people of the truth, *if* in fact they were really interested in knowing the truth. A person has to want to be led into truth, and God is a gentleman. The Holy Spirit will not lead a person into truth if they are unwilling to follow. We each have a responsibility to take a bite of truth, digest it, and go back for more. If we don't, we just end up ignorant. That's not meant to be mean or offensive, just a simple statement of truth. God has left us a book of truth, and He puts people in our path to share those truths with us; but if we stop up our ears and refuse to hear we can never claim ignorance as an excuse.

New Age beliefs tend to view God as a source of energy rather than a person, but that is not what the Bible teaches. GOD is known as **Father**, a person with a mind, will, and emotions. This person has a voice. He communicates with mankind. The Bible says in Genesis 1:26-28 that mankind is made in HIS image. In the image and likeness of God we are made - meaning, we each have a mind, will and emotions. We have a body. We have a soul. We are not just a lump of energy floating mindlessly around in the universe. No, we are people, made in the image and likeness of God. Every aspect of God whether in the form of Father, Son or Holy

Spirit is as a *person*.

God never represents Himself as someone He is not. He has emotions, He has feelings, character, integrity, standards, a value system, while energy does not. New Age beliefs tend to support ideas and philosophies that support independence from God rather than submission to a loving Father. They also support self-fulfillment, self-seeking, self-exaltation and making "self" their god. These beliefs support the an attitude of independence and rebellion, denying the Father that created us, yet believing we can become *like a god* without any relationship with Jesus Christ, Holy Spirit or the Father.

When I was young, my home life was very dysfunctional and oppressive. I came to despise the critical, stressful environment of my home. All I could think of was getting out from under control and being free to live the way I pleased. How I longed to live without rules! All I could think about was the day I could move out on my own. Finally, that day arrived. Freedom!

Suffice it to say, I lived like there was no tomorrow. At first I delighted in my new sense of freedom. Yet, sin took its toll and I felt the heavy weight of guilt, shame and emptiness. The life that I created for myself wasn't all I thought it would be. I had so despised the boundaries that had been set for me that I could not understand they were there to protect my spiritual, emotional and physical health. When people live without boundaries, it can be very easy to end up miserable and in bondage, and wonder how they got there.

God has set boundaries for us to keep us in the way of truth. These boundaries serve as a hedge of protection, but sin causes there to be holes in that hedge where demons can enter. Satan cannot defeat a person without them somehow granting the enemy permission. Satan always looks for legal rights. This can be obtained through generational sin through our ancestors, or it can come through our own actions. If we don't take the time to build a relationship with the Father, we will never understand His heart. We will miss His intention in why He wrote His word. God wants us to understand that those boundaries are for our protection, not to restrict our enjoyment in life or simply to be harsh. Any loving parent sets healthy boundaries for their children, and our Father is no different. If you are a parent, an aunt, uncle, or simply an mature adult, you can probably relate to what I am communicating. You understand that there will be times when your children don't agree with your rules because they lack maturity and wisdom to see certain situations from an adult perspective. In time, they often do come to understand why their parents had certain rules. Sometimes they don't even realize these things until they become parents themselves. Parents set rules to insure the safety of their children and to help them grow up into adults that have a proper sense of morality, responsibility and the wisdom necessary to govern their life. This is our heavenly Father's goal as well. His commands are not burdensome if a person realizes His heart is to love them and try to protect them from things that can bring trouble and heartache. Unlike natural parents, God never makes mistakes. He doesn't set rules just to be stingy or mean. He never acts impulsively or out of anger. He doesn't have mixed motives. His only motive is love. He has seen the end from the beginning and He knows how everything will play out before He ever wrote the script for our lives. If His word warns us that certain things are to be avoided, then we can trust that He knows it is not for our good. Demons, however, are always hoping they can tempt a person to do things that will leave them an open door.

Christianity promotes a humble Father/child relationship. A child's proper response to their parent is submission, love, and demonstrating respect towards their Father's wishes. A child that is disrespectful, stubborn and rebellious is naturally going to have a different sort of relationship with their parent than the one that easily honors their parent's wishes, but the parent doesn't love them any less. Our Father understands the pain and lies that people have endured to turn their heart away from Him, and He is very patient to try to get through to them. He repeatedly presents them with truth. That is one reason why we can trust that He is who He says He is, and He means what He says. One cannot argue with God and expect Him to change His mind. All religions and beliefs *do not* lead to heaven. The road to destruction is broad. There is only one way to salvation. God's word is His will, and He has made it clear. No one can enter into His holy heaven, or enter into relationship with Him outside of having a relationship with His Son. It is written,

"...nor is there salvation in any other, for there is no other name under heaven given among men by which we must be saved." (Acts 4:12)

"If you confess with your mouth the Lord Jesus and believe in your heart that God has raised Him from the dead, you will be saved. For with the heart one believes unto righteousness, and with the mouth confession is made unto salvation. For the scripture says, 'Whoever believes on Him will not be put to shame." (Romans 10:9-11).

In every other religion in the world, righteousness is self-made through good works, not imputed through a Holy God.

In every other religion, there is a demand to earn acceptance or favor to that particular god. In NO OTHER religion has man or idol given their life to redeem mankind from their sins. The Bible teaches us that we have no righteousness of our own. Ephesians chapter one is full of incredible truths about God's love, acceptance and redemption. Listen to this:

"He chose us in Him before the foundation of the world, that we should be holy and without blame before Him in love, having predestined us to adoption as sons by Jesus Christ to Himself, according to the good pleasure of His will, to the praise of the glory of His grace, by which HE MADE US ACCEPTED IN THE BELOVED!" (Eph. 1:4-6)

Wow! Total acceptance, unconditional love, all free for the asking. Did you notice that his entire purpose was to create us to be His sons and daughters? This is yet another confirmation through His word that the Creator of the Universe is simply madly in love with His creation – *you!* How awesome is it to be welcomed into the family of God? Does it change your perspective of yourself to know that you can become a child of the Most High God? How does it affect the way you see your future, knowing that you have access to everything in His house? It's true! As a child of God you become an heir, so everything that belongs to Him is yours, too. You have a Father that dearly loves you and wants you to experience the delight of knowing Him. He already knows you! It doesn't matter what you've done or how long you've been away. Like any parent, He just wants you to call Him and let Him know you're coming home.

Do you personally know Jesus Christ, having invited Him into your heart? If not, you can pray this prayer for salvation.

Dear Heavenly Father,

Right now I am making a choice to believe in what the Bible says. I reject all worldly philosophies and ask that you cleanse my mind of all confusion. I ask You to please forgive me of my sins and adopt me as Your child. I do believe that Jesus Christ is Your Son, that He died for my sins, and He rose from the dead. I believe He lives to give me the opportunity to know Him and live a victorious life. I thank you for forgiveness and the opportunity to know you personally. Holy Spirit, please fill me with the fullness of Your Spirit and empower me to live for Christ. Teach me how to enjoy a personal relationship with You. Tell me who I am in Christ. Thank you, Lord Jesus for being my Savior, my Lord, my provider, protector and friend. In Jesus name, Amen.

CHAPTER 4

THE RELATIONSHIP BETWEEN LUST AND WITCHCRAFT

Hopefully by now it is becoming more clear how the enemy works to entrap people and hold them in bondage. History has typically stereotyped the male as the predator, the sexual abuser or the molester, and the woman as the victim. However, none of these spirits that have been discussed thus far are gender specific. They can work through anyone. Sometimes the role of the abuser is reversed. The person least likely to be considered having a spirit of witchcraft operating in them is the very person that has become a captive of that spirit, and thus, a pawn the enemy can work through.

Both in scripture as well as occult books, it is the woman who is depicted as the image of seduction. The seat of all our appetites is known as carnal desire or our flesh. Carnal desire is also where lust has a place to manifest. Scripture tells us lust is never satisfied.[25] It knowns no limits and always wants more. Lust energizes the spirit of witchcraft.

One well known spirit of witchcraft is Jezebel. Although it is referred to in female form, the spirit of witchcraft can work through either a male or female. Witchcraft is the result of bitterness and rebellion. These spirits are given authority to oppress and influence those that are retaining bitterness. Those individuals have unhealed issues of the past that left them with feelings of anger, deep disappointment, and offense. Bitterness is unforgiveness that has been left unresolved for a long period of time. It is unfulfilled revenge; a desire for another person to suffer or pay for the perceived injury and pain they caused. The root of fear produces a desire to control others, because the person cannot bring themselves to trust God. When a person does not trust God, the only person they feel they can trust is themselves, and that is idolatry. That fear then becomes projected into every other relationship. Offense, unforgiveness and bitterness are open doors to the enemy, activating spirits of lust and witchcraft in the person's life. The person under this influence is often blind to it, but they have fear based

---

[25] Prov. 27:20, Prov. 30:15-16, Ecc. 4:8, 1 John 2:16

responses that manifest in the need to control others. This Jezebel spirit is known by its assignment. It wants control, and if directly stating their desires does not prove fruitful, they will resort to the use of guilt, shame, rebuke, pouting, turning a cold shoulder or silent treatment, ultimatums, manipulation, flattery, bribery, and pulling on other emotional strings in order to achieve their desire. This is the essence of witchcraft. It is to force the will of one person upon others until the person gets what they want.

Resorting to witchcraft tactics is the ultimate selfish agenda, for it completely disregards the will and desires of others. Loss of control can trigger extreme anger and emotional outbursts from someone that has this spirit operating in their life. On the other hand, this spirit knows how to flip the script and quietly strategize to achieve what it wants. Like a chameleon, it can change to adapt to just about any circumstance, and it senses exactly how to play to the emotions of others that it's trying to manipulate. This is one of the characteristics of this spirit that makes it so difficult to pin down. The difficulty is that the person is often blind to their need to repent. They rationalize things in their own mind that tells them their perspective is correct. Pride and rebellion are challenging to deal with and the root of all witchcraft. There are individuals that are blind to their own need to repent. Their hearts have become hardened, their emotions have become deadened and their minds are closed. A closed mind is a closed spirit; one that is no longer able to hear from God on their own. Pray for them to really *Manu* listen to what others are trying to communicate to them. Pray that they recognize their own need to change instead of being stubborn and resistant. Pray that they would realize their need to reject the attitudes and spirit of self-pity and accusation rather than shifting the blame onto others. We pray they realize they've been listening to the enemy's lies, and we ask God to deliver them from a victim mentality.

The truth is, God has made us to be overcomers in Christ. He will work all things for our good. He has also left us a promise that we don't have to live under a sense of condemnation – **if** we will walk **in the Spirit**, and not in the flesh.

"Therefore, now no condemnation awaits those who are living in Jesus the Anointed, the Liberating King, 2 because when you live in the Anointed One, Jesus, a new law takes effect. The law of the Spirit of life breathes into you and liberates you from the law of sin and death." Romans 8:1,2 VOICE)

When left unchecked, this spirit can multiply quickly. It can take over a family, church or larger organizations, and when it does, you will find those that operate in this spirit, and those that rebel *against* it. It always produces power struggles because people despise feeling others attempt to control them. Witchcraft is rooted in rebellion. Unhealed wounds of the soul can cause rejection to take hold in a person's life. When a person feels rejected they will strive all the more to receive praise and validation from others. A desire to be known can manifest through selfish ambition. This striving causes a person to try to be known or recognized through self-promotion and self-effort. A legitimate desire to be known by God is replaced by a counterfeit. There is a lie in the person's belief system that God doesn't see them or somehow has failed to validate their desire to be known, so the person tries desperately hard to receive validation and approval from outside sources. This is a false form of comfort and a deception, because only God can affirm our acceptance and validate our worth. While everyone can at times benefit from a word of praise and acknowledgment from others, our sense of identity or approval should not be solely based on what others think of us, or whether or not they acknowledge our talents, skills and abilities. Validation of who we are is received as a result of intimacy with the Lord. It comes as a by-product of spending time with Him and allowing Him to pour His love into our aching, empty hearts. The more we spend time with Him, the more we begin to realize that He *does* see us; in fact, He knows us quite intimately. The lies of the enemy that we have to strive for love, acceptance and approval are shattered in His presence.

"You, beloved, are worth so much more than a whole flock of sparrows. God knows everything about you, even the number of hairs on your head. So do not fear." (Matt. 10:30 VOICE)

Every single weapon the enemy uses against people is rooted in some form of fear. Every lie is based on some fear that the enemy hopes people will believe. **If a person is whole and emotionally healthy, the lies and the spirits attached to them would have no place to land.**

"Like a fluttering sparrow or a darting swallow, an undeserved curse will not land on its intended victim." (Prov. 26:2 New Living Translation).

One of the clearest biblical examples of lust and covetousness is found in 2 Samuel 11. It is the story of David and Bathsheba. David looked upon a married woman named Bathsheba while she was bathing on top of a rooftop. David was king. He had everything he could possibly desire, including as many women as he could want, but it wasn't enough. He coveted what wasn't his. David called for

Bathsheba, had sex with her, and when she was later found to be pregnant he conspired a plan to have her husband killed. The one thing Uriah had was his wife: Bathsheba. That was exactly what David wanted, and his lust knew no bounds. That is what made his sins even more atrocious. Uriah had faithfully served in the king's army, and he did so with integrity. David had him killed anyway, then guilt over trying to keep his sin quiet tormented his soul.

David was busy trying to carry on as though nothing was wrong but his heart refused to be quiet! His own heart condemned his sin and his soul was in torment. Fear and pride bound him to enormous guilt, shame and the fear of judgment. He couldn't bring himself to talk to God about it, so God did the merciful thing. He sent the prophet Nathan to confront him. Avoidance is never a viable option. Avoidance leaves people in a state of constant brokenness and separation from God. He can't heal what people hide, and He loves us too much to leave us in that condition, so He pursues us. Sometimes it is through the loving, probing questions of a friend, inquiring how we are doing, while at other times it may take a stronger approach to grab our attention. Sometimes it does take a strong message to break open a person's heart, especially if a person has been trying to avoid the conviction from the Holy Spirit for a long time. God loves us far too much to just leave us in agony of soul.

He will send someone to share a message of truth, because He knows that we will feel much better after we bring it to him. Confession cleanses the conscience of guilt and shame, and makes room for God to cleanse us from unrighteousness. It is far better to come to God willingly rather than wait for the consequences of our sin to catch up to us.

"For when I kept silent, my bones wasted away through my groaning all day long. For day and night your hand was heavy upon me; my strength was dried up as by the heat of summer. I acknowledged my sin to you, and I did not cover my iniquity; I said, 'I will confess my transgressions to the LORD,' and you forgave the iniquity of my sin" (Psalm 32:3-5).

"If we say we have no sin, we deceive ourselves, and the truth is not in us. If we confess our sins, he is faithful and just to forgive us our sins and to cleanse us from all unrighteousness. If we say we have not sinned, we make him a liar, and his word is not in us" (1 John 1:8-10).

The prophetic anointing is there to help lift people up, encourage them towards freedom and many other things, but people forget sometimes that God will have prophets confront people with their sin. A prophet's job is to deliver the message they hear from God. God hunts us down with the truth because His goal is not punishment; His goal is to redeem us out of the hand of the enemy. His goal is healing and restoration, but we must first acknowledge our sin and feel remorse towards that wrong action before we can be healed. Cleansing our conscience of guilt and shame comes as a result of obedience.

David had tried to avoid God and he suffered because of it. The penalty for David and Bathsheba's sin resulted in a curse, found in 2 Samuel 12:7-12. The child that Bathsheba bore to David died shortly after birth. God told David that adversity would be raised up from within his own family, and the sword would be upon house. Violence begets violence. The punishment is befitting of the crime. The laws of sowing and reaping are always in effect. That is also often a clue how to determine the nature of a curse.

David had been full of lust and covetousness, and that evil desire led to greater sins. Covetousness is a form of greed and idolatry.[26] When he felt he was losing control, he took matters into his own hands and committed the sin of murder. Let me draw a connection between a couple of different portions of scripture. I have never heard anyone

---

[26] Colossians 3:5.

connect these two different scenarios before, but they both illustrate the powerful influence of lust, and how it is connected to covetousness and witchcraft.

In many ways, David's sin was the same sin that Jezebel committed against Naboth in 1 Kings 21. King Ahab, Jezebel's husband, coveted a man's property. Naboth declined to sell it to the king. Ahab told his wife about it, and she set a plan in action to unlawfully take what was not theirs. They were thieves, but disguised their actions. Remember, lust is never satisfied, and covetousness wants what belongs to someone else. They were full of lust and covetousness, and they conspired to get what they couldn't have by any other means. They manipulated the situation, controlled the outcome and resorted to murder to cover their tracks. People lust, covet and murder to get what they want because they can't get it any other way. [27] The tenth commandment forbids covetousness because it is the root of many sins. If you make room for lust, covetousness is sure to follow, and shame is not far behind. It is a far bigger danger to people than most realize. In every biblical example of people that got carried away with covetousness, it led to far greater sins, and those sins brought on the judgments of God. Don't be seduced into thinking that it's ok to indulge in

---

[27] James 4:2.

a bit of immorality here and there. The enemy always has a plan to trip you into a pit that you can't get out of, so be wise.

The example in David's life also serves to point out the nature of a generational curse. Lust produces a desire for control, but the attempt to control others through the use of guilt, manipulation or other tactics is essentially the nature of witchcraft. People are either going to resist it and rebel against that spirit, or they will eventually surrender to it. That spirit often refuses to live peaceably with others because it always insists on its own way. The Jezebel spirit is one commonly referred to in the Bible. That anti-Christ spirit hates authority, but especially the authority of Christ in the believer. It rejects those it cannot control. That is why we are warned in Revelation 2:20 not to tolerate this spirit.

I want to interject something before I go any further. If anything I've written is speaking to you, please know that there is no shame in admitting when you're wrong. People resort to trying to manipulate situations all the time. They want what **they** want, because they feel they know best. Now, that could be related to any number of situations. It could be in the home, in a church situation or in the workplace. But, the reality is, we are not the most important thing! The truth is we don't always know what's best, we only think we do because we're only seeing a situation from our own perspective. We're supposed to honor one another, and to prefer others over ourselves. It's called compromise, respect, and humility. When people resort to those other tactics I mentioned, then they are operating in pride. Humility is the cure for worldliness and the spirit of witchcraft.

Humilty is the cure for the spirit of witchcraft

Sometimes people can see situations they feel should change or be handled differently, and that can make people impatient and anxious. One thing I've learned over time is that *God has a process* and a timeframe for each person, every church, and every situation to run its course. If we get impatient and try to take things in our own hands or try to implement our own solution outside of God's directives, we can make a mess out of things. Seducing spirits are always at work, trying to convince us to partner with the enemy's agenda. I can think of numerous times when the enemy spoke very insistently trying to convince me that certain situations would never change and I would be better off elsewhere. Had I acted on what I felt in my emotions, I would have missed a tremendous blessing. Be careful that lying spirits don't seduce you away from the blessing God has for you! Don't act impulsively, and don't act on frustration or other negative emotions. Wait for God to speak and give direction. When we try to handle situations ourselves, it can end up hurting ourselves and others.

"You may think that the situation is hopeless, but God gives us more grace when we turn away from our own interests. That's why Scripture says, God opposes the proud, but He pours out grace on the humble. So submit yourselves to the one true God and fight against the devil and his schemes. If you do, he will run away in failure." (James 4:6,7 VOICE Translation)

DEFILED BY BITTERNESS

Many years ago, I was in a church that was overrun by the Jezebel influence. Bitterness in the leadership and a strong emphasis on Old Testament teaching shaped the ideology in legalism, and it had made room for the spirit of religious control. Families were in turmoil because they were out of order. Men didn't seem to understand how to operate as the priest of their home, and the women were trying to wear the pants in the family. No one was submitting to anyone and the power struggles had a ripple effect throughout the church. Everyone wanted to be in charge and it caused a lot of offenses. There was also a very strong spirit of lust on many of the people there. Lust and sexual immorality is a trademark of the Jezebel spirit.[28] It was a mess! It always will be when a demonic presence is

---

[28] Rev. 2:20

involved. Again we recognize the connection between lust, sexual immorality and the spirit of witchcraft. Demonic spirits work in groups, so if there is one that is recognizable, then there are probably other spirits that also need to be addressed. Anyone with a spirit of witchcraft and divination should not be ministering to others because there is a demonic spirit speaking through them. That spirit is anointed to defile others, cause offense, and create more wounding. This defilement will cause disappointment in both God and others that causes people to rebel against God. The enemy always tries to create a sense of bitterness and disappointment in people because that is how he turns people away from God. If he can produce bitterness, then he can release witchcraft as well, because all witchcraft is produced from bitterness and rebellion.

"Rebellion is as sinful as witchcraft, and stubbornness as bad as worshiping idols. So because you have rejected the command of the LORD, he has rejected you as king." (1 Sam. 15:23 New Living Translation)

There are a couple of related stories in the Bible that I would like to mention. The first one is found in Acts 8:9-24. It's the story of Simon the sorcerer. The followers of Jesus had been scattered because of persecution, but the gospel, along with signs and wonders, was spreading like wildfire.

One man by the name of Simon, who had been a well-known and powerful sorcerer in the city, watched the disciples closely and followed them around. He was so impressed that he, too, decided to get saved. But, what he desperately coveted was the power of the Holy Spirit. That was lust fueling his desire, and Peter discerned the wrong motive. This was a superior power to the devils Simon had served, and he knew it. Simon offered to purchase the Holy Spirit, who was the source of the miraculous power he kept witnessing. Peter, however, rebuked him and told him that Holy Spirit was not some sort of magic that could be purchased with money. He told Simon,

"You aren't even close to being ready for this sort of ministry! Your heart is not right with God. You need to turn from your past, and you need to pray that the Lord would forgive the evil intent of your heart. I can see deep bitterness has poisoned you, and wickedness has locked you in chains." (Acts 8:2-23 VOICE)

I don't know what Simon went through in his life to experience such pain and disappointment, but over time it obviously turned to bitterness. Bitterness comes from deep wounding, disappointment and then a rejection of forgiveness towards those that had caused the pain. In every situation where there is witchcraft, there has to first be the events that led up to the person feeling rejected, unloved, betrayed, full of fear or some other source of deep pain and disappointment. Unresolved pain and lies in the belief system regarding those feelings and situations cause a person to embrace anger, a desire for vengeance, jealousy, and other wickedness. Simon got saved, but he was not yet delivered of all the demons that had been a part of his life. This led to a motive of selfish ambition in his desire for ministry and a wrong motive in asking to purchase the Holy Spirit. The *ways* of God were foreign to him. There were still many evil spirits that manipulated his emotions, hindering his ability to truly understand God. And so it is with many of us. The worldly ways still cling to people long after they are saved. It takes time and dedicated effort to embrace the determination it takes to work towards healing and freedom, and freedom only comes by allowing God to show us why *our* ways are wrong. It takes humility for people to recognize when they have the wrong spirits motivating their desires. Lust helps fuel those wrong motives. For those who feel called to ministry, there must be a process of time, inner healing and personal growth before they are prepared to minister to others. Therefore, the Lord will wait until a proper sense of humility and sanctification is present in His vessel before He releases them into a place of public ministry.

Bitterness and witchcraft always work together.

These spirits collaborate to defile not just one person, but many. The spirit of bitterness will also cause people to pick up the offenses of others. The spirits of bitterness and witchcraft are anointed to defile through words. That is why scripture tells us not to fall short of the grace of God. In other words, don't let your heart become so hurt or angry that in the process you lose your sense of understanding, compassion, grace or kindness; if you do, the enemy is waiting to take advantage of you. Offense is like far reaching vines that are attached to the root of bitterness. They reach out, grab hold of their victim, and defile their host, creating an ongoing ripple effect of bitterness and offense in others.

"See to it that no one comes short of the grace of God, that no one be like a bitter root springing up and causing trouble, and through him many become defiled." (Heb. 12:15 NET Bible)

The Apostle Paul also encountered a woman with a spirit of divination (witchcraft) but he was able to discern the spirit working in her life. Although she spoke the truth, it was by the wrong spirit, which had an assignment of flattery and distraction against Paul and the work he was sent to do. He rightly discerned the spirit at work and cast it out. He didn't try to compromise with it! From these examples, we understand the necessity of appointed leadership having discernment to recognize the spirit of those among them. The enemy always looks for a way to come in unaware. It is so important not to befriend the wrong kind of spirits. If we do, then we give them place to operate in our lives, or potentially in a congregation.

1 John 4:1 reminds us to test the spirits because that will help us discern its source. We have been given an anointing to know the truth.[29] Whether or not a person has a personal relationship with God is shown by whether or not they live in the truth, obey His commands, and live in the light. The person who truly has God hears the truth. They are receptive to it. If they do not hear and continually reject truth, then the spirit of the world is upon them and they are living in spiritual darkness.[30] The Holy Spirit is a discerner of truth because HE IS THE SPIRIT OF TRUTH. He testifies to the type of spirit operating in others. [31]

It takes discernment to know when something should be handled relationally with counseling, and when the problem requires a different approach. **Witchcraft does not respond to counseling; it is subdued by binding the strongman.**

[29] 1 John 2:20.

[30] 1 John 3:4-8

[31] 1 John 4:6

[32] Sexual immorality is also a very strong influencing factor. It may not always result in the physical acts of adultery, but because it is a seducing spirit and known as an 'immoral woman' in scripture, the danger is to seduce people away from the straight ways of the Lord. Sitting under leadership that tolerates these spirits can also become an open door for lust, the perverse spirit and other spirits such as incubus and succubus to affect those that are submitted to that leadership. What affects the head will affect the rest of the body. There is a curse that goes into effect for tolerating Jezebel. It includes sexual immorality, sickness and death. We know this according to scripture in Revelation 2:20-23. We are not called to compromise with any form of idolatry and witchcraft; we are called to eradicate it.

The Jezebel spirit is a very religious spirit. In the Bible, Jezebel was a Phoenician wife of King Ahab. She was a liar, a thief, and a murderer. She also called herself a prophetess, but Jezebel came by way of her knowledge through demonic spirits, not the Holy Spirit. She hated God's prophets and swore to destroy them. Her commitment to that end was so great she made an oath to her god Baal. She vowed to exchange her life for the life of God's prophet, Elijah, if she didn't make good on her threat to have him

---

[32] Mark 3:27

killed! That is how devoted this spirit is to the destruction of the prophetic voice in the church. Satan hates true prophetic authority because it gives life, breath, revelation, strategy and direction to the body of Christ. It also exposes what is of another spirit and out of order. Jezebel had an anointing, but it was not from a holy source. It was an anointing to defile and destroy. Jezebel threatened the prophet Elijah and got him to quit his calling.[33] She seduced him into giving up, using intimidation and fear. The enemy is sly! Don't let the wrong voice lure you into giving up your mantle, authority and calling, because that is always the enemy's goal. We are warned not to believe every spirit but to **test the spirits**, according to 1 John 4:1.

You'll find the story of Jezebel throughout the book of Kings in the Bible. Her father was Ethbaal of Tyre, King of Phoenicia. The Phoenicians worshipped many gods and goddesses but their chief god was Baal. Baal was the god of fertility and agriculture over the Canaanites. Ethbaal was probably a high priest for Baal. Part of the culture of that day involved sex in front of their idols, as the people believed it could cause them to bear more children and be fruitful. The Israelites belonged to God and were forbidden from practicing polytheism (the belief and worship of many gods).

---

[33] 1 Kings 19:4, 15-17

They were also forbidden from participating in sexual orgies or using sex as a form of idol worship. The other nations surrounding them *did,* however. Sex was used as an offering and a form of worship to false gods in exchange for knowledge, conception, prosperity, and to empower their gods. Sex was used to raise the energy level to empower a spell. Spells are used to take something by force that one cannot seem to obtain on their own. The one who is praying to their god (or casting a spell) uses their emotions to send out a force of energy powerful enough to cause their desired end to come to pass. Understand that 'energy' alone is insufficient. What is really happening is word curses and soulish prayers are sent out where demons act on them to try to bring them to pass. If people have carelessly left open doors to the enemy through sin, then demons have the ability to do what they have been assigned to do. The Bible warns us that life and death are in the power of our words. We don't want to empower demons to carry out curses by careless speaking. Bitterness and negative speaking are equally involved when it comes to empowering a spirit of witchcraft. **Witches, wizards and others who practice occultism have understood the relationship between sex, lust and demonic power for many thousands of years.**

Lust is not just sexual. A spirit of lust is a consuming

desire for power, sex, money, fame, recognition, influence or dominance. Envy and covetousness go hand in hand with lust. Many times lust can work hand in hand with selfish ambition. Lust and selfish ambition lead to idolatry because 'self' becomes the one who is being worshiped. Feeding the idol of lust can become all consuming. It also invites the perverse spirit. Do you see how it can become a very tangled web of demonic spirits? When dealing with deliverance issues, it's important to allow the Holy Spirit to communicate. The information He reveals sets people free from self-deception. Otherwise there is the strong possibility that spirits that have been evicted will come back and bring even more spirits back with them. Before you know it, you've got an even bigger mess.

"When an unclean spirit comes out of a man, it passes through arid places seeking rest and does not find it. Then it says, 'I will return to the house I left.' On its arrival, it finds the house vacant, swept clean and put in order. Then it goes and brings with it seven other spirits more evil than itself, and they go in and dwell there; and the final plight of that man is worse than the first. So will it be with this wicked generation." (Matthew 12:43-45, Berean Bible)

The way to protect oneself from the enemy coming back in after deliverance is to be filled with the Holy Spirit. It is so important to fill that void with God. Prayer, worship, acts of service and good, wholesome relationships are all part of filling a person's life with things that lead to a greater sense of purity and fullness. The things that led up to bondage in the first place must be cut off. Wrong relationships must be cut off. There must be a strong commitment to avoid certain temptations and make sure that porn and other unfruitful fantasies are no longer tolerated.

At this point you may be wondering why there's so much explanation about witchcraft. Perhaps you're thinking, "I thought this was a book about lust and being set free from condemnation and shame from sexual sins." It is, but **the door to lust doesn't always come open in the most obvious way**. People seem to think that lust comes in through porn or watching the wrong sort of sexually alluring things. While those things can certainly be true, that is not always the case. Many times, as in my experience, the door to lust was strongly connected to some form of witchcraft, idolatry and generational rebellion. There was also a generational root of bitterness that took many years to heal. Unforgiveness issues lingered and kept coming back, which left open doors to the enemy. At the time, I did not understand the connection between the different issues. I have also found those who struggle with sexual demons also have links to bitterness, jealousy, or a background that includes false religions and witchcraft. They are not always separate and distinct issues; they are usually interconnected. Therefore it becomes necessary to offer an explanation that helps others understand the relationship between all these spirits, because getting free involves dealing with more than just bad habits. Obedience and confession of our sins is really the only protection we have. We must close all the doors so that the hedge of protection God has for us doesn't have holes in it.

Lust is connected to the perverse spirit. A perverse spirit is a mixture, it's impure. According to the online Free Dictionary, the word **perverse means**:

1. Willfully determined not to do what is expected or desired (contrary);

2. Obstinately persisting in an error or fault; wrongly self-willed or stubborn;

3. Marked by a disposition to oppose or contradict;

4. Turned away from what is right, good and proper; wicked or corrupt

5. Similar words indicate a negative personality, one that is resistant to guidance or discipline; one that has a negative outlook on life, lacking in integrity or moral conduct.

In the Hebrew, it is defined as "to bend, twist, knot or

distort; also, to make crooked, to change or depart. The Greek describes it as corrupt, to misinterpret, wrangling and constant arguing, curved, winding and strange. (In the Greek, 'skolios" is also the root word of scoliosis.) From these definitions, we can understand that the perverse spirit is responsible for many things. It twists truth, brings confusion and is also responsible for false doctrine, in addition to the sexual element.

None

There is a very strong link between Santeria, Lukumi and demonic sexual spirits such as incubus, succubus and lust. I have also written on this subject in my book, **Healing the Heart of a Nation**. Some portions of this text are taken from that book.

Witchcraft spirits are not discriminatory. They will look for any door that is open to them. If you suffer from demonic oppression in dreams or at night with sexual spirits, there is a strong possibility that some form of the occult power of witchcraft, voodoo, hoodoo, Santeria, Lukumi or other connection to the occult that is causing those things to occur.

Santeria and Lukumi are forms of voodoo that merge the spiritual practices of people from Cuba, Puerto Rico, the Dominican Republic (who were also Roman Catholics), Haiti and tribes from West Africa. Centuries ago, slave traders sold captured members of the Yoruba tribe to the Spaniards as slaves. The slave owners baptized the slaves into Catholicism as a forced religious conversion. "As a result of the fusion of Francophone culture and Voodoo in Louisiana, Creole African Americans associated many Voodoo spirits with the Christian saints known to preside over the same domain. Although some doctrinaire leaders of each tradition believe Voodoo and Catholic practices are in conflict, in popular culture both saints and spirits are believed to act as mediators, with the Catholic priest or Voodoo Legba presiding over specific respective activities. Early followers of Voodoo in the United States adopted the image of the Catholic saints to represent their spirits."[34] "Other Catholic practices adopted into Louisiana Voodoo include reciting the Hail Mary and the Lord's Prayer." [35] Since the slaves could not worship their own gods openly, they pretended to be devoted to the Catholic saints, but they were actually worshiping their own gods. They are like parallel religions that exist side by side, hidden within the Catholic religion. Santeria is a Spanish word but originates in Cuba. It is estimated that somewhere between 75-100 *million* people are a part of this growing religion.

---

[34] Jacobs, Claude F. & Andrew J. Kaslow (2001). The Spiritual Churches of New Orleans: Origins, Beliefs, and Rituals of an African-American Religion. University of Tennessee Press

[35] Nickell, Joe (2006). "Voodoo in New Orleans". The Skeptical Inquirer.

Everything in Satan's kingdom is a counterfeit of the kingdom of God. Santeria and Lukumi have many rituals and ceremonies that are held in a house temple, or what is called a 'house of Saints.' The meetings are conducted by Priests or Priestesses. There is a display of 'thrones' that represents the kings, queens and deified warriors who are invoked for guidance and blessing. The 'disciples' of Santeria are given prayer beads as a sacred point of contact with the spirits called upon in these witchcraft ceremonies. After many rituals are performed, the person is 'born again' into the faith. Not the faith of God, mind you, but of the occult. In many of these traditions, parents bring their children before an occult priest or priestess for initiation into the occult.

"The slaves simply renamed their gods using the saints' names and continued with their old worship. The blending of these two religions became known as Voodoo in Haiti and the islands to the south and as Santería in Cuba and the islands to the north of Haiti."[36] "The old Yoruba faith was maintained intact with only a superficial sheen of the saints overlaid to pacify the slave owners and later the Christian government and culture."[37] Those that practice this religion

---

[36] Gardener, Cult of the Saints: An Introduction to Santeria; The Llewellyn Journal.

[37] ^Gardener, Cult of the Saints

identify as sons and daughters of their 'supreme being' known as Olodumare. They have a 'trinity' in their godhead also, but they are all Satan in one form or another. The same false gods of Santeria and the Yoruba religions are known by various names of the Catholic saints. Listed below are the dual identities by which these pagan saints are known.

- **Yemaya/Mary, Star of the Sea**.
  Yemaya is the African Mother Goddess. She rules over the oceans, the moon, women and children, fishermen and sailors, witches, and secrets. The belief is that all life comes from Yemaya the sea. She is associated with the Virgin Mary in two of her aspects: Our Lady of Rule and Mary, Star of the Sea. Mary is known and worshipped under many titles and is the corresponding saint for a number of African gods.

- **Obatala/Our Lady of Mercy**
  Obatala is another aspect of the pagan "Divine Trinity." Like Yemaya, he is associated with the Virgin Mary, this time in the aspect of Mercy. As the first-born of the gods, Obatala is regal and wise. He blows away negative energies and resolves ethical issues. As Yemaya is the patron of mothers, Obatala is the patron of fathers.

- **Chango/Saint Barbara**

  Chango is the third member of the pagan trinity. He is the god of transformations, the god of thunder and lightning. Chango is invoked when a person seeks revenge on his enemies, and Saint Barbara is patron of wrongful death. Lightning is a potent symbol for both the Catholic saint and the Santería god, and both Chango and Saint Barbara are prayed to for protection in storms.

- **Eleggua/Saint Anthony**

  Eleggua is known as Legba in the Haitian faith, and sometimes as Eshu. As patron of doorways, Eleggua's place in the home is by the door to protect the home from any negativity. Saint Anthony is also known to be a finder of lost things and a worker of miracles.

- **Osain/Saint Joseph**

  Osain is the god of the forest. He is the patron of all healers and herbalists. Some people bury statues of Saint Joseph on their properties to "leave a blessing" for the next occupant or property owner. (Obviously, this can leave a curse instead of a blessing).

- **Oshun/Our Lady of la Caridad del Cobre (Our Lady of Charity)**

  Oshun is another goddess worshipped under the umbrella of the Virgin Mary—in this instance, Our Lady of la Caridad del Cobre, patroness of Cuba. As the love goddess, Oshun rules pleasure and sexuality, marriage and the arts, but she also oversees all money matters.

- **Oggun/Saint Peter**

  As the god of war, Oggun is belligerent and combative, and the patron of human effort. Saint Peter is petitioned for success and employment.[38]

There are many more 'saints' that are used in Catholic prayers as well. Please let me be clear that what I'm communicating is not about bad mouthing the Catholic church or those that belong to the Catholic faith. It's about exposing spiritual practices that bring defilement and invite a demonic presence in people's lives. The only way to set people free from deception is to arm them with truth. This mixture involves Voodoo practices that are also connected to the perverse spirit and lust. Santeria and Lukumi are occult

---

[38] ^Gardener, Cult of the Saints

practices that involves invoking spirits by calling on the names of these pagan "saints." Prayer candles and statues of Mary or other saints are a common practice in constructing altars to summon these spirits. The Catholic church does not openly admit to any association with Santeria, Lukumi and its sister religions. The problem is, many of those who *do* practice these things consider themselves to be members of the Catholic church. Demons don't differentiate between whether a person identifies with Santeria, Lukumi or Catholicism. They simply look for whether or not someone has granted them legal grounds to access their life. Forbidden practices such as praying to anyone other than our heavenly Father through His Son Jesus Christ is a sure way to do that. The reason this is wrong is because ONLY Jesus Christ gave His life to be a mediator between God and man. Only Christ shed His sinless blood to redeem mankind from their sin. He is the only one who has a legitimate right to be the door to our Father. Jesus said that all those who attempted to go through a different door were considered a thief and a robber.[39] When people break God's laws and try to go around His prescribed order, demons are then free to torment, harass or put a curse in effect.

---

[39] John 10:1

Catholics do admit they pray to various saints. Many of these saints were real people who attained sainthood status after they died. However, it doesn't matter how good a person is or *was*; nowhere in scripture are we advised to pray to other people, living or dead, or to make our petitions to them. Perhaps those who are in heaven do pray for us. Romans 8:34 tells us that Jesus is at the right hand of the Father interceding for His people. It is not a stretch of the imagination to think that those in heaven would be praying for those on earth; however, we are never told to pray *for* people who have passed, or *to* the saints. We are not ever advised to pray through those who have passed on. We are to pray to the Father through His Son, Jesus Christ. Jesus himself told His disciples how to pray (and who to pray to) in the Lord's prayer (See Matthew 6:9). According to 1 Tim. 2:5, there is only one mediator between God and man, and that is Jesus Christ. Anything else is a form of conjuring and divination. African and Cuban cultures hid their true worship behind the faces of the saints, but others, such as those in the Catholic church that pray to various saints, *are* committing the same sin. When praying to any other name instead of Jesus, the face of that 'saint', idol or deity is Satan himself.

Earlier in the chapter I mentioned the need for discernment, and to 'test the spirits.' The problem with these practices and traditions is that they are teaching a different sort of message that includes religious witchcraft. The Bible says 'what does light have to do with darkness?' Yet these beliefs and practices have been embraced as though they are compatible with Christian values. Many people are unaware of the fact that the doctrines of the Catholic church are compromised. Their mixture of forbidden practices such as praying to the saints, praying ritualistic prayers, or looking for absolution through a priest instead of the blood of Jesus opens them up to a curse. The pope and at least some of the bishops are viewed as infallible when it comes to their teachings, and become a substitute 'voice of God' to their people. The word 'infallible' means incapable of making mistakes or being wrong. Faultless, flawless, impeccable or perfect. So, the Roman Catholic Church is essentially saying the pope is God. Obviously, this is clearly wrong. At the very least it is considered idolatry to elevate man in a position equal or higher than God, and that leaves anyone that practices these religious traditions at risk of being under a curse. The perverse spirit, voodoo and witchcraft spirits will affect their lives, whether or not they realize that is going on. These spirits make room for demonic sexual spirits as well. They often go hand in hand. Other religions can also be at fault for believing in false doctrines and invoking the spirits of false gods. To be fair, there are a variety of churches and religions that want to present themselves as Christian but have actually departed from the ways of the Lord. The difference is seen in their ideology.

"But even so, the Spirit very clearly tells us that in the last times some will abandon the true faith because of their devotion to spirits sent to deceive and sabotage, and mistakenly they will end up following the doctrine of demons." (1 Tim. 4:1 VOICE)

The reason I went into a lengthy explanation is because Catholicism is another common denominator when it comes to issues related to incubus and succubus spirits. The roots of these religions produce a very strong connection between lust and sexual spirits, and are quite prevalent in the African-American, Cuban and Spanish ancestry. I have had various people with Catholicism in their background ask for help with these spirits, including a minister in the Catholic church. **A person doesn't have to actively practice witchcraft for it to exist as an unbroken curse, and those things can still be affecting families even today.** The practices forbidden by God and the spirits associated with them are not part of a pure gospel. Things that have been introduced by man and 'added to' the Word of God as though it came from God are man's traditions and a different doctrine. This produces a mixture and a perverse spirit. We are never to alter the scriptures. This is an effect of a perverse spirit. It twists truth.

People who can be quite sincere in their desire to worship God can be sincerely *wrong* in what they've been taught. They may be in a religious system that has altered truth and they never realize that they are partaking of a doctrine that carries a curse. Both God and demons are not interested in our excuses. Either they have legal grounds to be there or they don't. Demons count on people being ignorant of how they work, but it's my hope that I can help shed light on some of these things so that people can avoid those pitfalls.

"I testify to anyone that adds to the prophecy in this book: if anyone adds to them, God will add to them the plagues that are written in this book; and if anyone takes away from the words of the book of this prophecy, God will take away his part from the tree of life and from the holy city, which are written in this book..." Rev. 22:18,19

"Do not add to His words, or He will rebuke you and prove you a liar." Prov. 30:8

Jesus warned us in His word that the traditions of man have the power to nullify the word of God in our lives. When that occurs, a person's faith is severely constricted and compromised through the doublemindedness that is produced. God's word tells us that He is pleased by *faith*. Real faith is not settling for the form of religion, but seeking the person of Jesus Christ. It is getting to know our Heavenly Father and Holy Spirit. Each person of the trinity wants to be deeply connected to us in personal relationship. Religion is just a form that has no power to produce intimacy with God. It is a counterfeit and a substitute for actual relationship with the Lord and his Holy Spirit. Those outward religious practices grieve the Holy Spirit because they are a replacement for intimacy and relationship with Him. If we will seek His presence through thanksgiving, praise and worship, we will encounter Him. When we encounter the Holy Spirit, He guides us into the truth that can make us free. It's not just the receiving of truth, it's embracing it and allowing it to have it's perfect work in our life. That is what sets us free.

You now have a better sense of how lust, witchcraft, and sexual spirits work in connection with one another. Billions of people are influenced by some combination of demonic spirits. I've told you what witchcraft is, how it works, and the damaging effects those spirits can have on individuals, families, churches and society. Those that can discern these spirits may tend to think that those who have these spirits in their life are an enemy or someone to be avoided. While that may sometimes be true, that is not true in every case. Sometimes the reason those people show up in your life is so you can be an agent of healing.

When God first started talking to me about the need to break generational curses, He began by telling me to renounce Voodoo. At the time, I had no idea that it existed in my family. As I was obedient to renounce it, Holy Spirit began to reveal things that up until that time had remained hidden. The enemy knew about it, however, and was taking advantage of our blind spots. Suddenly, Holy Spirit started to connect the dots and many things began to make sense. Each time He showed my husband and I something new, we would take time to pray over it and renounce those sins that originated in our bloodline. It is very important that both spouses work together in these things so that they are able to break the cycle for good.

As one who was once bound by fear, lust, witchcraft, bitterness, and shame, let me explain the more human side. The deep pain, shame and rejection that people experience is sometimes so unbearable that they feel they cannot take one more day on this earth. I talk to so many of them that feel there is *something wrong with them* or they would not continuously experience rejection. They don't understand why they continuously deal with repeating cycles of discouraging problems. The lies and rejection they feel are so hurtful that they can't discern that the problem isn't necessarily with them; they've been marked by the enemy and he's trying to destroy their life. When a person constantly suffers and struggles because of curses in their life, the grief from those things causes a sense of hopelessness. I have talked to many that are on the verge of despair, some even praying that God would end their life because they cannot take any more pain, shame and fear from the demonic torment. They desperately need someone to explain that God loves them and has not rejected them. Their circumstances are in opposition to the truth and many are baffled because they simply haven't been taught how to get free. The pain and frustration they experience is due to demonic spirits attached to their lives. What I hope others understand is that many of the people who contact me *are* Christians – brothers and sisters who do love God but have not been delivered, and *they are suffering*. They are so tired of the pain and sorrow of feeling abandoned by God. The enemy has convinced them that their Father does not love them, so they end up blaming God instead of blaming the devils that have them bound. All they understand is that their life is marked by deep emotional suffering and spiritual poverty. They want relief but don't know how to obtain it. Without a compassionate healer, they remain stuck. This is why the church must be equipped to help them. For a person to feel they are unaccepted, unloved and covered in shame is a deeply troubling pain in the psyche that drives people to despair. It is a broken heart in the worst way. My husband and I understand this pain because we've lived it. There are souls all around us in dire need of someone to help them uncover the lies and get free. They need teachers and prophetic voices to show them their true identity. They must be led into a place where they can find rest for their Spirit, comfort for their aching heart, and hope for the future.

While we need to be discerning and wise about the spirit operating in others, we also need to demonstrate compassion and grace. Individuals bound by bitterness and witchcraft often cannot recognize about themselves what others see about them. They may know they are up against spiritual warfare and witchcraft coming against them, but often they cannot understand the reasons why. Many people cannot discern that it is also coming from *within* them. There is some unknown open door that the enemy is using to take advantage of them. Of course, there are going to be those who are so hardened in their sin that they no longer have the desire to be obedient to God. On the other hand, there are also those who are genuinely miserable and crying out to God, wanting relief from their tormenters. *Discern the difference*, and remember how generously God extended grace to you when you called on His name. Great is His mercy! We are clothed with a mantle of forgiveness so that we can share the good news of forgiveness with others, and offer people a fresh start. May each of us enter into the new day that God has waiting for us. He has a gracious provision for a new beginning.

.

CHAPTER 5
THE WAY OF ESCAPE

Many people may have questions about how to deal with the temptations of sexual urges, loneliness and singleness. We are, after all, human beings created with the desire for intimacy. Our bodies produce hormones that trigger certain urges and longings that are beyond our control. Those are legitimate needs based on how we are created. Lust, however, is driven by selfishness and is fueled by a demonic spirit whose assignment is to take people into captivity. It is challenging enough to subdue natural desires. It becomes even more difficult when the enemy has a person bound by demonic oppression.

Everyone needs to learn how to possess their own vessel so that they can maintain a sense of purity in their life. Every craving or urge will eventually pass. In the midst of sensing a temptation, remember that the seduction of the enemy is like the voice of a siren. It wants to lure you into deep water where it can drown you. That is its only goal. Temptation is there to construct a barrier between you and God, and if you're married, it's there to place a barrier between you and your spouse as well. Ask yourself what it is you really want. Force yourself to say it. Don't let that seducing spirit continue to talk to you and stay in your head unchallenged because that is just entertaining the thoughts. The longer it stays, the more you will find yourself reasoning with the temptation and finding ways to justify acting on that impulse. Instead, hear yourself saying, "I acknowledge how I'm feeling right now, but what I really want is _____." Then, take authority over the influence of the enemy. Combat the temptation with truth. You can say something like, "Satan, stop tempting me with an illegitimate way to have this need filled. It is written that I am to flee sexual immorality according to 1 Corinthians 6:18. It is also written, *"there must not be even a hint of sexual immorality or impurity or greed,"* according to Ephesians 5:3. Furthermore, it is also written in Ephesians 4:27 that I am *"not to give the devil a foothold."* I resist your temptation and I command you to leave me now in Jesus name." Remember that true desire is fulfilled through relationship with the Lord. If you will dedicate yourself to falling in love with Jesus, He will help fulfill the desires of your heart, which is hardwired to need intimacy with God.

"Whom have I in heaven but You? And there is nothing on earth that I desire besides You." (Psalm 73:25)

It is the responsibility of every individual to learn how to say no to temptation and work out their salvation with the Lord. I realize for those that are seeking balance, that is probably an inadequate and simplistic answer. I cannot tell others how to manage their sexual desires. Each person must learn how to ride out the temptation until it passes. What I do know is that God has promised that when temptation comes, He will also provide a way of escape.

"No temptation has overtaken you that is not common to man. God is faithful, and he will not let you be tempted beyond your ability, but with the temptation he will also provide the way of escape, that you may be able to endure it." (1 Cor. 10:13 English Standard Version)

Focus on finding other outlets. Service to others is often a good place to start, because it takes the focus off of self and puts it on helping others. God has promised that when we face a temptation, He will also provide a way of escape. The way of escape involves humility, confronting pride and fear that hold a person hostage, and actively resisting the enemy. The question each person must answer for themselves is whether they will take the method God has provided as their particular way to escape temptation.

People cannot truly live free and healed until their past is destroyed. The only way this is possible is through Jesus' death and resurrection. Salvation is for everyone that will receive Christ as their Savior, but ministry that truly liberates people from the demonic attachments in their lives is specifically for those who are saved. It is not for the unsaved. Many people only want to be free from demonic tormenters but still want to live without a relationship with God. It does not work like that. Jesus said that healing is the children's bread in Matthew 15:21-28. Christians can have demons, but God has provided a means of helping people obtain their freedom.

The ability to live free from spiritual oppression and torment is our portion because we are children of God. Galatians 4:5-7 tells us that God adopts us as His children, thereby giving us full benefits as an heir. We are no longer slaves, and should never settle for living as one. The spirit of shame tries to force people into giving up their inheritance of freedom and remain in captivity. The lie of the enemy is that by acknowledging the sin and asking for help, a person will be put to shame. That is a lie. God's word tells us,

"No one who hopes in you will ever be put to shame, but

shame will come on those who are treacherous without cause." (Psalm 25:3 NIV)

"They looked to Him and were radiant, And their faces will never be ashamed." (Psalm 34:5 NIV)

Allow me to bring up another point. If people have a fear of being put to shame, then it is probably tied to a memory from their past, where they are subconsciously relating to a previous situation. Ask Holy Spirit to show you what situation or memory is tied to the fear of being put to shame. I recently did this and was surprised how easily the Lord showed me several situations from my early childhood where I had been deeply embarrassed because of something that others did to me. None of those situations were actually caused by wrongdoing on my part, and therefore I was not to blame. Realizing that the enemy used those things to get a hook in me and cause me to feel that same fear allowed me to see the situations objectively, pray about them, and release them.

No one who seeks the face of God and turns to Him for freedom will be put to shame. He doesn't turn away the one that comes to Him. The enemy knows this and tempts people to trust the lie, believing that the only place of safety is in hiding the sin and keeping it secret. The enemy works in darkness. He can be very convincing to keep people believing in the lie. No one truly wants to live as a slave, but shame is a very powerful emotion that has the ability to keep people trapped through fear. Face the fear head-on. It's the only way out of the chains. If you remain a slave to fear and the enemy keeps you from asking for help, what is the eventual outcome? What is the worst that can happen? Sin and bondage will always result in some form of brokenness, loss, and destruction. The enemy's only job assignment is to destroy. It might end up being your reputation, your marriage or the loss of respect. Now, ask yourself if you are willing to pay that price. On the other hand, if you face your fear and ask for help, what is the worst that can happen? You might feel momentarily awkward or embarrassed to talk about your problem, but anyone that is truly an anointed servant of the Lord will not shame you. They will not condemn you, for they too, understand that we have all needed help getting free from one thing or another. They will do their best to help you, and you will have gained your freedom. Ask Holy Spirit to send you to the right person that will understand your needs. Holy Spirit is kind and compassionate to those who are hurting and bound, yet, He is a force to be reckoned with towards the spirits of darkness. He is there to set the captives free!

Transformation doesn't happen automatically. We still

have to drive the enemy out. Sometimes the enemy takes up residence in a person's flesh, their thoughts, or specific places in their body. Some people have struggled and wrestled with God for what seems like a very long time and they are exhausted from all the effort. Demonic spirits can be hard taskmasters. I remember being angry and frustrated with God, blaming Him for being a hard taskmaster because it felt like I could never get a break. I was worn out from the battle. It was a struggle to hold on to my faith and a struggle to maintain a sense of faithfulness towards God. I felt like I was stuck and frustrated most of my Christian walk and I couldn't understand why everything seemed so incredibly difficult to maintain any sense of peace and joy. Because I lacked understanding, I got angry I blamed Him for what I was going through. What I didn't understand at the time was the fact that it was Satan that was the hard taskmaster, and it was his lying spirits that continually accused God in my thoughts, driving a wedge between us. This was the root of bitterness that kept growing back. I felt like I was in a wrestling match most of the time. This was due to a root of bitterness that kept growing back.

Listening to those accusing thoughts caused me to begin to speak negatively out of my own misery. This allows a spirit of self-pity to come into a person's life. Self-pity comes as a result of feeling as though you have been treated with injustice. Bitterness comes from hard servitude and disappointment. The person feels that God has rejected them and does not love them. The victim in turn feels anger and more pain. Bitterness and self-pity are very strong, stubborn spirits. When you hear a chorus of complaints rising up within you, stop yourself before it comes out of your mouth! The voice of the accuser is Satan. Satan creates the problems then blames it on God. He wants people to speak those accusations out of their mouth because it puts them in agreement with him, (and the spirit of rebellion), giving him legal grounds to gain more strength in that person's life.

During those times of frustration, the mental and emotional torment became unbearable. I felt overpowered by grief, partly because of circumstances but also because my accusations against God allowed the enemy more room to torment me. In the midst of my pain, I cried out to the Lord. He was not about to entertain my pity-party or my accusations! He told me to rise up and fight the enemy, and to watch my blind spots. It was sort of like a slap in the face, but I had been out of order. I humbled myself to the Lord by confessing that I had blamed Him wrongly, and asked His forgiveness. Then I took authority over the enemy and commanded him to go! Immediately, the tears and the spirit of torment left me. I was amazed that it could happen that fast! This is experiencing the reality of God's word in James

4:6,7. If you practice it correctly, it works every time.

A demonic presence such as lust, bitterness, self-pity or other things work to separate us from the intimacy and relationship of love with our heavenly Father. The voice of the accuser will always lead a person away from God and bring separation. One cannot accuse God of being unfair or failing to do His job properly and still be in right alignment with Him. Separation is the first thing that happens.

The second thing that happens is accusation places a person in rebellion, thereby giving the enemy legal grounds to bring torment, grief, depression, or any number of things. That is why we must be diligent to guard our heart and confess our sins quickly so that the enemy cannot find an open door. Asking God for forgiveness places the blood of Jesus over that door so that the enemy is shut out. According to James 4:6-7, God resists pride, but He gives grace to those who are humble. That is just another way of saying that He gives us His help when we put our attitude in check and come to Him the right way – with humility. When we are truly submitted to God, then we can stand on the promise in verse 7, resisting the enemy and he must leave us. If we're resisting and he's not leaving, then the enemy sees an open door that we cannot see for ourselves.

The question is, "What benefit do you receive from allowing demons to be in charge?" Sometimes, whether the person recognizes it or not, demons serve a purpose in helping them to avoid something that feels uncomfortable or undesirable. Is there something that you are trying to avoid dealing with in your life? Are you using a false form of comfort to try to escape stress or emotional pain? Remember what I mentioned in an earlier chapter: All addictions are rooted in a need to feel loved, valued and accepted. Do you believe that God loves you and can give you a new perspective on an old issue? Do you believe that you can trust Him to show you something that will take the pain away that is connected to certain events and memories? If so, then what is causing you to choose the lie, the pain, and the bondage? When people avoid facing truth, then what they have chosen for themselves is willful blindness and the torment that comes with it.

The truth is, we can trust Holy Spirit. He is gentle, gracious and has absolutely no motive to hurt us. None. He does not use shame as a tool for discipline. He is there to unlock our chains and lead us into freedom. Will it require obedience on our part? Will it require humility and a willingness to submit to His leadership? Yes, but we can be confident in facing the future because we know who holds the future. We can trust God to lead us into circumstances that will be more healthy for us. We can face whatever we need to face because He has promised to never leave us or forsake us. If you can learn to look at the thoughts, feelings, and situations in your life through the lens of objectivity instead of emotions, it will help you see the way of escape. That is one reason why we must depend on Holy Spirit to show us. It comes by facing reality instead of trying to avoid it. It also comes from choosing the option of legitimate comfort that God has provided through relationship with Him.

If we choose *not* to trust God for the answers we need, then the energy expended in feeling upset, angry or resistant to God actually serves to build an altar to the enemy. Complaining and wanting to insist on having our own way builds the wrong sort of altar in our life. People probably don't stop to think about that, but who wants to build an altar to the enemy? All it does is give demons added strength to pull people deeper into rebellion. Demonic spirits are empowered to carry out even more assignments against people and their families.

I understand what it feels like to want to believe God for His promises but still remain stuck. There are spiritual principles that WILL release breakthrough.

Surrender is the key to freedom. Many people have such

difficulty trusting the Lord because they are suspicious and fearful of losing control. They don't know what to expect or what the Lord will require of them. I understand that struggle between wanting to trust God, yet still wrestle with yielding total control. It took me many, many years to realize that I still had open doors to the enemy. I didn't recognize what they were. In various ways self was still enthroned in my heart. I was still working through trust issues with the Lord and wrestling with surrendering my fears, frustrations and insecurities.

Freedom comes as a result of obedience. There is just no way around that. Let me draw your attention to something.

*"And the Lord's bond-servant must not be quarrelsome, but be kind to all, able to teach, patient when wronged, with gentleness correcting those who are in opposition, **if perbaps God may grant them repentance leading to the knowledge of the truth, and they may come to their senses and escape from the snare of the devil, having been held captive by him to do his will"*.** (2 Timothy 2:24-26).

Notice that there is responsibility on behalf of the Lord's servant, but also to the one receiving from them. I emphasized a portion of the above scripture because the bottom line to escaping the snare of the devil is for people to 1) come to their senses, and 2) repentance. The only way a person can come to their senses is to be led into the truth. This requires solid teaching of the word of God, and an understanding that God really does mean what He says in His word. He doesn't adjust His word or His spiritual laws based on how a person feels about their level of obedience. He doesn't give preferential treatment or go easy on things that He has said are wrong. He will never go easy on sin because He hates it. He knows the harm that it will do to people, even if they don't always understand or agree with Him.

Part of being led into truth is through learning how to have an intimate relationship with God. We give our love, worship and heart over to Him, and He reveals the truth that makes us more and more free. Receiving truth is to receive a change of perspective, which then has the capacity to lead us to a place where we can 'recover our senses' and decide to make a course correction. That is the part known as repentance. But without intimacy with God, how can we hear what He has to say? Intimacy is key to healing and freedom because that is where God reveals the answers to the questions of our heart.

As we are quiet before Him and listen for Him to speak, we can then receive His loving thoughts about us. He tells us who we are in Christ. He reveals our dominion and heritage as a child of God. Often the key to deliverance from one issue is directly connected to healing of a heart issue. The key to freedom is tied into our perspective of what it means to walk in true humility and submission to God's Holy Spirit. We all need to work with Him to heal the belief system because it affects our identity. When the identity and wound issues are healed it often helps a person regain a different perspective over other things. A changed perspective often has the capacity to change the mind – and that is what is known as true repentance. A change of heart changes a person's behavior. This is key to breaking the power of oppression in people's lives.

"You have rescued us from dark powers and brought us safely into the kingdom of Your Son, whom You love." (Col. 1:13)

The gospel message has been preached for thousands of years. It has proven that it is sufficient to bring people to repentance. The beauty of the cross is the message of hope that it brings, for God has promised that once we confess our sins, He chooses to remember them no more. The good news of forgiveness is powerful enough to convict the heart and bring people out of darkness and into God's kingdom. We believed the message we heard about Jesus and the cross, and it was enough to compel us to pray a prayer for salvation.

Permit me a little rabbit trail here. Many years ago, when I was trying to get free from drinking, I had come to believe the lie that I heard in recovery programs. The twelve steps are actually very spiritual principles, and many people find tremendous help through them. I am grateful they do, but I had real difficulty with the constant need to identify with the person that I had come to despise. I realize that not everyone has the same experience as mine, but I found the meetings I attended left me with overwhelming depression. I couldn't stand the thought that I would always have to think of myself as an alcoholic and found no relief from the guilt and shame that were continuously with me. I didn't want to identify with that. The good part about treatment programs is that they force the person to acknowledge their sin and take responsibility for it. The bad part is they don't offer a legitimate remedy for sin to take away the guilt and condemnation that weighs heavily on the conscience. The groups I was familiar with never brought Jesus into the picture, so it was like trying to get help in a program that talked about God in a round-about way but didn't ever tell you how to connect with Him. Every time I attended a recovery meeting, I was forced to identify with the sin, guilt and condemnation of my failures and the things that brought me shame. I found no hope in any of that. These are lies spoken against a person's true identity in Christ, and those lies keep a person chained to the past. I would feel so depressed I would go right back to the bad habit all over again. Recovery programs declare abstinence as a way of life, but they don't deal with deliverance. Many other groups for a variety of addictions offer suggestions and advice that has no power whatsoever to change the person's core beliefs or deliver them from evil spirits. The attitudes and practices governing these programs, unless the person truly finds Christ, leave people under the heavy weight of bondage and still living with the same demonic attachments that oppress them. The problem with all of this is that **our old identity is directly linked to shame and sin.** If we want to be truly free, then we have to let the person we used to be before we got saved die. We don't try to keep making a better version of the person we used to be; we realize that is not who we are today because in Christ we are reborn into a new creation. [40]

Jesus set me free, but I had to first recognize the stronghold of lies in my belief system. The errors in my belief

---

[40] Galatians 2:18-20

system continued to spin the lie that I would never be completely free. As long as I continued to believe the lie, I continued to slip up and resort to occasional drinking. As I continued to grow in Christ, however, realizing that I could break that unholy alliance resulted in my eventual freedom. I had to come to accept the truth that God said about me. It required me to grow in the knowledge of truth and actually embrace it. Lust, lies and other temptations all originate from the same place and must be dealt with in the same manner. As with any sin, it must be confronted with the truth of God's word.

I remember the hope I first felt upon hearing the good news of the gospel. I heard someone say that I never had to feel hopeless ever again, and I never had to feel that kind of shame again. I couldn't believe it was true. That little seed of hope began to stir in my heart. If that Jesus they talked about was real, I wanted Him. I had lived without hope for so long, overdosing repeatedly and hating my life; once I heard the good news, I had to know Him! I was so desperate to leave the person I had become and my old life behind. I knew I needed a fresh start and a new identity! When you truly despise your sin and are ready to become a new person, the gospel message really is great news! Do you remember when it first became good news to you? It can be again! That is when you recover your strength, take a stand

and resist the enemy, and command him to leave. Devils leave when they know you're actually submitted to God and in right alignment to Him.

Once again, it is time to look into God's word and search for the message that will convict the heart and compel us to repent from whatever we have been doing outside of His will, and turn back to Him. It may be a wrong belief that puts us in agreement with the enemy instead of being in agreement with faith. It is God that delivers, not man. Do not put your faith in ministers. Keep your eyes on Jesus, the author and finisher of your faith. Set your hope on Him. He is your liberator! Looking back at the scripture in 2 Tim. 2:24-26, we see that it is God that must grant a person repentance. He has looked down the corridor of time and seen the end from the beginning. He knows those that will genuinely repent and do His will, and He knows those that will not. Those that choose to live in obedience to His will are the ones that are delivered and set free from their captivity.

Perhaps you are thinking, "I don't know if I am ready to surrender complete control. Does that mean I must remain stuck in captivity?" Yes and No. Healing and freedom come in steps and stages. That is how He works with everyone. He is so gracious and kind. God knows our thoughts and our struggles, and He takes pity on His children. He works with us and helps us understand that we really can trust Him. Little by little, as He reveals things to us, we are given the choice to receive more truth and walk into it. If we decide to reject the truth that can make us free, then we obviously remain in bondage longer than if we had chosen to accept what He communicates and work with Him to obtain another level of healing and freedom. He will let us stay in whatever stage of wounding we choose for ourselves. The Lord loves us and wants us to trust Him enough to let go of the things that He knows are harmful to us, but He leaves that choice up to us. He doesn't violate our will. He *does*, however, require a person to part with their sin in order to obtain healing and freedom.

If we will confess our wrongdoing then He is faithful to cleanse us from unrighteousness that comes as a result of sin. Confession of sin and prayers of renouncement means that we agree that sin needs to go. There needs to be an acknowledgement on the part of the individual that indicates they want to change. It means turning away from those things that God calls sin and recognizing the value of purity. Embracing purity is to leave behind the things of the world that got a person in captivity to the devil in the first place.

Some may ask, "What if I don't know what to confess?" It's simple. Ask Holy Spirit to show you. I remember one day

I came to a red light and there was a truck with big letters in his back window that said, "Repent Now!" I gave a little laugh and thought it was a bit vague. Repent...of what, exactly? I said out loud, "Well, I appreciate this person's zeal for you Lord, but how can a person repent if they don't know what to repent *for?*" Instantly a thought came to mind about a situation I had completely forgotten about, and I knew that was the Lord's way of telling me I needed to make it right. At the time, our finances were being robbed through all kinds of bank fees and I knew there had to be an open door somewhere, but I couldn't pin point it. When the Lord brought that particular memory back to mind, I knew instantly what He wanted me to understand. So guess what? I did my part and He did his. The thief instantly got shut out once the situation was corrected. Holy Spirit knows the things that are leaving open doors to the enemy. Don't be afraid to ask Him to reveal the problem!

STUBBORN SPIRITS

There are some demonic spirits that are so stubborn and resistant that it feels like one can never get completely free. Demons have a way of revealing weaknesses and character flaws. If you think of someone you don't much care for or you're offended with, and something rises up within you and says, "I am not going to forgive so-and-so," you've got spirits of Unforgiveness, Defiance, Stubbornness and Rebellion at work. If you tend to justify certain behaviors or attitudes that are less than becoming, you might be dealing with a stubborn demon. If you feel stubborn and defiant towards God or genuine repentance, then that is a clue you have a very stubborn spirit at work in your life. It can come in through generational sin that runs in families, or it can be doors you've opened yourself but the reality is some spirits are stronger that others and thus become more difficult to remove from one's life.

Matthew 17:18-21 is a warning about stubborn spirits that don't give up easily. Jesus advised fasting along with prayer to help move the demonic spirit out of a boy when the disciples could not cast it out. When they brought the issue to Jesus, He told them that it was because of their unbelief. They were dealing with a stubborn spirit that did not want to let go of the child, and they became frustrated at their lack of understanding.

I struggled with a stubborn root of bitterness all my life. I could tell it was a generational spirit because it affected our whole family. I never even met my grandmother but I know she had to have had it too, simply by observing my own family members and hearing stories about how she treated my mother. Poverty was generational. Addictions, lust, rebellion, mental and emotional illness were also quite strong in my family. All of these were the tell-tale signs of a demonic root system at work. Idolatry and witchcraft were strong and deeply rooted. It felt like I was never going to get truly free. When a person has struggled for a long time with the same recurring issues they get weary, discouraged and unbelief sets in. Hopelessness sets in. This can cause a person's faith to begin to fail, and they may become offended with God. They don't understand how to get free and may get angry all over again. The person may even feel like giving up on God, but unbelief must be challenged!

FASTING is a chain breaker. It helps break up the entangled root system so that it can be removed from a person's life. Especially when you're dealing with a generational spirit that has seemingly been with a person all their life, FASTING is a necessary component to help drive the enemy out! Couple it with worship, prayer, declarations of faith, and decreeing God's word. It might not get completely taken care of the first time or two, but if you remain persistent and determined, you can and WILL get free. The added component of fasting is the strategy to see the enemy defeated in your life so that you can be free and healed. You may also need to have an anointed minister pray over you.

Demons work in groupings but they have to follow the chain of command. The strongman is in charge, similar to a general of an army. One the strongman is bound, he is forced to comply with the minister operating in the authority of Christ. Once the general is subdued, command all spirits under his command to leave their host. If you don't get the general, you'll continue to war without results because he just keeps strategizing with the troops. The lesser demons gain strength to resist deliverance from the strongman. Fasting humbles our flesh and allows our Spirit man to rise up and take authority over the enemy. Fasting, high praise, worship, declaring God's word and making decrees against the enemy are powerful and effective tools against the enemy. It is like taking a huge hammer against the works of darkness. Every time you bring the hammer down, you are weakening Satan's grip and destroying his demonic network.

"Is not my word like fire," declares the LORD, *"and like a hammer that breaks a rock in pieces?"* (Jer. 23:29 NIV)

If you have to fast three days out of every week and repeat the process of praise, declarations, repentance and renouncing the sins of your ancestors, do it. Keep repeating the process. As you do, your spirit man gets stronger and the enemy gets weaker. Eventually your spirit man will overcome and force the enemy to let go and vacate!

One cannot fight and expect to win against an enemy (whether externally or internally) if they are in agreement with the same spirit(s). For instance, if you agree with the lie that you are rejected, you can't evict it until you confront the lie with truth. You must break agreement with it. Demons are demonic entities with a personality and character traits. They must be addressed similar to how you might address a person. For instance, if you recognize a friend on the street and you want to get their attention, you would call out their name. If you are yelling the wrong name, they may not realize you're speaking to them. Addressing those spirits by name, whenever possible, helps identify them specifically and command them to obey the authority of Christ. For example, you must tell them, "Rejection, I am no longer in agreement with you. The word of God says I am accepted in the Beloved. You are a liar! I break every agreement I have had with your lies and I renounce any covenants and contracts that have been binding in the spirit realm. In Jesus name leave me now!"

The reality is we cannot defeat any enemy unless we are in proper alignment with God and have taken care to annihilate the enemies in our past. One way to freedom is to incorporate fasting along with prayer, praise and worship, and declaring God's word. Transformation can only take place to the degree that we are willing to own the sin of ourselves and our ancestors. We must reverse the curse!

Every temptation has a lie connected to it. Once a person realizes that, it becomes easier to resist the enemy and recover their will. Demons want us to believe that they are in control and that we cannot be free. The reality is that they are simply finding ways to keep truth away from us so that we continue operating out of a lie-based belief system. Emotional pain is rooted in what we **currently believe** about God, ourselves, past events and our future. Keep hammering away with God's word until truth settles the argument in your soul. That is when those spirits are forced to let you go.

The Holy Spirit within you has more power than you realize. You are not a victim unless you choose to be. You do not need to feel helpless in your situation, you just need a different perspective of how you see it. Ask God to help you understand from a spiritual perspective and give you the strategies to outwit and overcome your adversary. God is trying to get the body of Christ to mature and understand that they must use the authority He has given them. As you cooperate with God in your own deliverance, you become stronger. Many times, as with any addiction, you get free *when you decide to be free*. **Demons love to offer people counterfeit solutions to try to solve their problems**.

Every time a person succumbs to the temptation to turn to their bad habit, it is because they are trying to escape something either within themselves or in their environment that they are trying to avoid. So what is it? It could be stress, anger, frustration, an inability to cope or something else, but resolving the WHY of what compels you to turn to a counterfeit means of problem solving is very important. Understanding your WHY will help you recover your will so that you can exercise your authority against the enemy. Don't let the enemy help you solve your problems, because reaching for the temptation offered by the enemy doesn't resolve anything! It only tightens your chains. Remember, he can only control you if – either by cooperation or through ignorance of spiritual laws – you are in agreement with him and you provide him opportunity.

Victory comes when you truly exercise your dominion over the enemy. You have to get down to the core belief – something that is rooted in your past experiences – that reveals why you feel the need to try to fill a void in your life with some illegitimate source of comfort. When a person has pain in their life many times it can be traced back to some lie in their belief system. If you don't deal with the lie, it's only a matter of time before something else manifests as another unwanted behavior. I'm not saying there won't be a struggle to regain your freedom, but persistent resistance and honest repentance go a long way towards obtaining your deliverance. There will be times when you do need an anointed minister to lay hands on you and command the enemy out, but at other times you can get free by working directly with the Lord.

A friend of mine works with people using the Transformational Prayer Ministry (TPM) model developed by Edward M. Smith. This model teaches that current emotional pain is directly related to lies that a person believes. The lies are formed as a response to experiences in the person's history. While in prayer, the person identifies the feelings related to current distress. The brain automatically takes the person to memories where those feelings were experienced. The beliefs related to those feelings are identified, and then the Lord is invited to bring His truth to the specific beliefs that are lodged in the memory. Once those beliefs are replaced by the Lord's truth, the enemy no longer has a nest in which to build his stronghold of lies and he has to leave. As the lies are removed, true loss may be identified and the Lord is able to carry away the grief of that loss.

Resolving childhood wounds and negative events that have accumulated over time with truth allows a person to respond to current situations from a different perspective. When Holy Spirit brings truth to the memory where the lie was formed, it is truly transformative! There is nothing more powerful than God's voice directly to the individual. Holy Spirit is able to change a perspective in a moment, precisely at the point of need in the memory, in a way no human can ever achieve. A new experience is implanted in a person's history! This encounter with Christ in the memory leads to mind renewal and transformed living which is automatic and free from self-effort. A person receives effective breakthrough and a great relief in current life.

My friend describes her experience in this way, *"Inner healing such as TPM is one avenue God uses to rewrite my history. I can see where He is in my history. I have landmarks of His presence, touch-downs in crucial times of my life. My story becomes a history book of His presence in my life – from the beginning until now. And my perceptions of myself and my circumstances are infiltrated with Him...Today, when my thoughts go elsewhere, when my fears drop me off a cliff, my history with Jesus snaps me back to Him. I am His again, resting in the experiential knowledge that He is my reliable, safe place, custom made for me!"*

Whether the person you are trying to help is yourself or someone else, you might consider asking the question, "Where in your history does this feeling seem familiar?"

"What happened?" and, "What did you believe about that event or memory?" Why do you believe that? Then, ask the question, "Does what you believe line up with the truth in God's word?" If not, then you have just uncovered a lie in the belief system which you can then counteract with the truth of scripture. Invite the Holy Spirit to bring His counsel. What do you hear God saying about the matter? Pray over those things and ask Him to speak about that particular experience or memory. When He speaks and reveals truth, the power of the enemy's lies is broken. Getting down to the core belief tied to certain events and memories is key to healing. It's not always what happened at a particular time in your life, as it is about your <u>current belief</u> concerning those things. It's what you believe *today* that is causing you pain. Revelation from God unearths the lies and shatters them. You are not how others have diagnosed you. You are not the labels that others have placed on you. **You are who God says you are, and His word settles the matter.** There is nothing more powerful than God's voice directly to the individual.

Healing the past goes beyond transforming core beliefs that are tied into certain events and memories. That is a huge part of it, but in the cases of generational sin that has left the door open to the enemy, it's not *our* memory or any event that we are aware of that holds the necessary clues. We have no way of knowing what doors to the enemy our ancestors have left open that the enemy is still using against us today. Therefore, the information will be much more difficult to identify. That is where we need to take steps of faith to seek the Lord as well as actively partner with God in self deliverance. This is done through prayers of renouncement and repentance on behalf of ourselves and our ancestors. That is why both methods of healing ministry are vital. The revelation and teaching on identity is also crucial to the life of the believer because it implants new thoughts, beliefs and understanding into the individual. This type of revelation truly remakes a person from the inside out as their belief system changes.

I believe what is needed is a paradigm shift in how we have done ministry in the past. It's not either this *or* that, it's a gathering of various streams of ministry together to provide an upgrade in the way we approach helping others. No one approach is better or more effective than another. We need the TPM approach to help heal the lies and core beliefs that have twisted our perception of God, ourselves and others; but we also need prayers of renouncement to cleanse our past from generational curses. We need powerful revelation and teaching on identity, and prophetic ministry to know what God is saying to others. When we bring these anointed streams of healing ministry together, I believe it will produce a far more effective prototype for ministry. When we honor the gifts and wisdom God has put in others, there is a blessing that takes place. It's where the oil flows. This is a time for **ministry partnership**. It's about building effective teams so that the blend of various anointings, spiritual gifts, skill and wisdom blend into a diverse mixture, producing a higher level of ministry efficiency.

CHAPTER 6

HOW PERVERSE SPIRITS AFFECT MARRIAGE

AND FAMILY

Sexual demons are quite serious, as all demons are, in their intent to destroy marriage and families. Reflect back on what I wrote in an earlier chapter on the perverse spirit. It creates conflict because of its intent to war against anything good, moral and godly. It is a warring spirit that fully intends to take captives.

What many couples don't understand is that not everything they've been dealing with are natural issues related to communication, intimacy or other situations common in marriage. In many cases, especially where there is evidence of lust, pornography, infidelity and other things wreaking havoc in a marriage, it's due to the deliberate interference of an invisible third party that is attempting to fuel relational breakdown until the marriage collapses. The enemy's voice is the seducing voice of temptation, jealousy, suspicion, accusation, fear of abandonment and much, much more. If people take the bait, eventually it will cause strife, wounding, resentment, alienation, rejection and shame. It is time for people to understand the undermining presence of demons that have been assigned to destroy their marriage and family. *Forgive one another.* Do your best to work through your differences quickly. Your spouse is not your enemy; the enemy is your enemy. Satan's goal is to divide marriages so that the couple has no power of agreement. That way the enemy can withstand their prayers. It's time to unite against the enemy so that those demons can be shut out. Where two of you are gathered in Jesus' name, whatsoever you agree upon in prayer shall be done for them.[41] The enemy works to prevent unity wherever possible so that a couple's prayers lack strength.

Countless numbers of marriages are destroyed by porn, affairs, and sins of the flesh. Yet, many marriage counselors as well as many Christian books written on healing marriages from these issues fail to address the need to sever demonic attachments Porn, for instance, is not just a bad habit. It can easily become an addiction and an

---

[41] Mathew 18:19

obsessive-compulsive disorder. One clear indicator that demonic activity is involved is when the person no longer has the ability to control their behavior. That is because a strongman is in control. While there will always be a need to address topics such as communication, accountability and ways to rebuild trust, there is an equal if not greater need for healing the soul through the liberating ministry of the Holy Spirit. Healing the soul of things such as rejection, inferiority, unforgiveness and other issues helps to eliminate the wounds the enemy uses to gain an advantage.

Demons, especially incubi and succubae, are very jealous for the object of their desire, which could be one way the spirit of jealousy and control also affects people in relationships. A spirit of witchcraft can act as a temptress to seduce one or both spouses into having an affair. It can also interrupt reproduction, cause sterility, miscarriage and sexual dysfunction. These spirits will create suspicion, jealousy, and stir up strife. Demons wage war between spouses so that they can become the one to provide the (illegitimate) sense of comfort and sexual satisfaction. The more a person participates, the more they are bound.

When one of the partners in a marriage gets involved in porn or other ungodly fantasies, it can create a sense of anger, distance and rejection within the marriage. The other partner can tend to feel as though they have been cheated on. Frequently the male is the one to turn to these things. For some men, porn offers a more exciting option than the motherly view they have of their wives. Sometimes what pleases one spouse is not necessarily what pleases the other, and porn and unrealistic fantasies seem more interesting than the routine of the familiar. Men tend to be visually stimulated by certain imagery more so than women. These fantasies also offer a false sense of comfort to those who are lonely or overcome with physiological and natural desires. Men also turn to these things because they look for the mental and emotional stimulation that gives them the rush of endorphins. The majority of married men are not looking to have an affair. They don't necessarily want to go down that road that leads to bondage and other objectionable behaviors, but they end up getting addicted to the rush that gives them the endorphins. Endorphins produce a sense of euphoria, pleasure and a calming effect. There are a variety of reasons why people use porn, ungodly fantasies and engage in other sexual behaviors, and many of them contain a sense of risk. For some, it's the risk factor that seems to make it appealing, knowing that they are partaking of something that is secretive and forbidden. Each of these behaviors can be equally damaging to reputation and relationships. For some women, it's as emotionally damaging as though their husband did have an affair. The damage that lust and porn have on a marriage, family and children can be disastrous and devastating. Each person suffers in a different way.

Making a marriage work takes continuous effort, even in the best of marriages. Men's needs and women's needs both sexually and relationally are different. It takes time to build a healthy relationship. Sometimes the burden of what it takes to build a healthy relationship can require much more of a man than he feels capable of giving, and it's easier to opt for self-gratification. For some men, it becomes far more effort than they are comfortable with to communicate their sexual needs, their need for intimacy, and to be understood in a relationship. It can feel so foreign and difficult that they try to avoid it altogether and end up going through the motions, without any real sense of satisfaction. There are two different things going on with men; their sexual needs and relationship needs. They either make the effort to combine those needs or they separate them. For some men, those two areas of his life may not even be on the same page. That is not the case with women. Women's sexual and relational needs are very much intertwined. Women want to feel loved. While they don't expect men to solve every problem that frustrates them, they do want to be heard and understood, and they want to feel secure in the relationship. Men and women have many of the same needs, but not necessarily in the same order of priority. Men look for a strong sense of affirmation and respect. Their sense of feeling loved is directly connected to the level of respect and affirmation in the relationship. While men do enjoy a sense of physical connection, their need for intimacy is not their primary need as it is for a woman. Men connect more through physical contact while women connect more through words. Unless a man truly understands his wife's needs, and the wife understands her husband's needs, the marriage will lack strength. It is so important to grow together. Factors such as age, appetites, physical appearances and other variables all play a part in the ever-changing aspects of marriage. Love thinks about giving, but lust thinks about getting. Love is focused on the other person, while lust is focused on self.

"In his book *The Drug of the New Millennium, the Brain Science Behind Internet Pornography Use*, Mark B. Kastleman provides a very detailed description of the process that takes place inside a pornography viewer's brain." [42]

"In order to understand these processes, the author first

---

[42] Alex, 5 Brain Chemicals in Healthy Sexual Act and How it is Different from Pornography Addiction; Brain and Addiction, Free Recovery Course, Treatment Program for Porn Addiction, Nov 1, 2010, retrieved online Jan. 18, 2017.

examines how the brain is designed to work in a healthy sexual relationship. Then he compares it to brain activity during the pornography viewing session. He describes both processes as "going down the funnel". The top of the funnel represents our normal state of mind, where we are completely present and aware of what is going on around us. As we begin to engage in a sexual activity, our attention span begins to narrow down, until the sexual climax is reached. After that, we begin to slowly return to our normal, wider view of the world.

In a healthy marital relationship, sexual intimacy creates powerful physical, emotional, and chemical changes:

- **A Narrowing Process**: The married couple enjoys a wide perspective of the world and the people around them. Then, as they become physically intimate, their brains begin to narrow in focus. Climax is the most narrowly and powerfully focused singular event that the brain can engage in. To make this happen, the brain must narrowly focus its attention and block out all distractions (work, the children, paying bills, etc.)

- **The Release of Natural Chemicals**: To aid this narrowing process, the brain begins releasing a flood of endogenous (meaning produced from within) chemicals. These natural chemicals include the following:

- **Dopamine**: Elevated levels of dopamine in the brain produce extremely focused attention. This chemical causes each spouse to focus intensely on the other at the exclusion of everything else around them. A release of dopamine is associated with craving and dependency in addiction, which may be why it can help produce a healthy attraction and dependency between the spouses.

- **Norepinephrine**: This chemical generates exhilaration and increased energy by giving the body a shot of natural adrenaline. Norepinephrine has also been linked to raising memory capacity. Whatever stimulus is being experienced in the presence of this chemical is "seared" in the brain. This helps explain how a couple in love can remember the smallest details of their beloved's features.

- **Testosterone**: Testosterone is known as the hormone of sexual desire in both men and women. For men, however, it is the key hormone of desire, triggering feelings of positive energy and well-being.

- **Oxytocin**: The flood of oxytocin at climax acts as

a natural tranquilizer, lowering blood pressure, blunting sensitivity to pain and stress, and inducing sleep.

- **Serotonin**: This natural chemical is released right after climax, bringing on a deep feeling of calmness, satisfaction and release from stress. Anti-depressant drugs like Prozac are designed to increase levels of serotonin.

The Experience is More Than Just Physical: There is more to the experience than just chemicals released in the physical body. The mind, heart and spirit are all joined together. The final crescendo is a culmination of all the things husband and wife have shared – doing the dishes, paying the bills, raising the children, all that make up a marriage.

A pornography viewer goes through a similar process as couples in a marriage but the involved chemicals produce a completely different result. "...Through pornography viewing, the physical and chemical processes are virtually identical to those in marital sexual intimacy, but with some radical differences.

- **A Narrowing Process**: Before beginning to view pornography, the individual enjoys a wide perspective of the world. "...The porn viewer begins blocking out distractions – but he is blocking out much more. He is alone. The object of his narrowing is pornographic images. Details of daily life, such as work and paying bills, slowly fall into disarray as the person starts blocking out all thoughts of God, his marriage, family, morals, commitments, and consequences...

- **The Release of Natural Chemicals**: The porn viewer's brain begins releasing endogenous chemicals. The viewer feels highly aroused – all of the stress, pressures, anxieties and pain in life begin fading away as his system is flooded with endogenous drugs. The viewer is able to self-medicate and escape the reality of life.

- **Dopamine**: Elevated levels of dopamine in the brain produce extremely focused attention. This causes the viewer to focus intensely on the pornographic images at the exclusion of everything else around him.

- **Norepinephrine**: This chemical induces feelings of exhilaration and increased energy by giving the body a shot of natural adrenaline. Norepinephrine also increases memory capacity. This explains why porn addicts can recall viewed images with vivid clarity years later.

- **Testosterone**: Pornography triggers the release of testosterone which in turn increases the desire for more pornography.

- **Oxytocin**: Oxytocyn acts as a natural tranquilizer. The individual seeks an Oxytocin rush to cope with the stress and pressure of life.

- **Serotonin**: The release of this natural chemical evokes a deep feeling of calmness. Individuals turn to porn to self-medicate and escape the stress.

The Experience is More Than Just Sexual. There is a lot more going on in the pornography experience than sexual arousal. In fact, if you remove sexual arousal from the process, any similarities to sexual intimacy in a healthy marriage would cease. "...A tidal wave of conflicting and confusing images and messages wash over the viewer. Visual images are stored as emotional memories in the brain before the logic center realizes what has happened. When the logic brain catches up, it brings on a "fight or flight" type response. The adrenaline gland sends out cortisol, the "stress hormone," which in turn activates myriad body-system processes to counteract stress. In essence, the entire pornography process is intensified and supercharged, far beyond what sexual arousal alone would accomplish. The human system is not designed to deal with this overwhelming level of conflicting stimulations. **This is why many neuropsychologists refer to pornography as "visual crack cocaine".**

An Empty and Hollow Climax: When one uses pornography to reach climax, the brain desensitizes to the images, habituates to them, and eventually becomes bored. An increase in the variety of images and/or time spent on the Internet is required to maintain stimulation levels. In a healthy marriage relationship, sexual intimacy is only a part of everything else going on in the couple's life. So when the couple "brings all of that into the bedroom," it is highly unlikely that the brain will habituate to the sexual process.

When Reality Returns – the Hopeless Dialogue: When the porn viewer emerges from the narrowest part of the funnel back to a wide perspective, the heartless "drug-high" of pornography and climax quickly dissipate. Suddenly his rational thinking returns and the hopeless dialogue begins: "What have I done? What was I thinking?" He wasn't thinking; that was the problem! Once he descends into the Pornography Funnel, he gives up his ability to "think". The overpowering flood of chemicals overrides his cognitive thought and reasoning abilities. The frontal lobes – the logic center of the brain – are virtually shut down and the limbic system, which controls the pleasure/emotional center of the brain, takes over." [43] (Kastleman, pgs.39-57)

---

[43] Alex, 5 Brain Chemicals in Healthy Sexual Act and How it is Different from Pornography Addiction; Brain and Addiction, Free Recovery Course, Treatment Program for Porn Addiction, Nov 1, 2010, retrieved online Jan. 18, 2017.

We know the Holy Spirit wants us to live a pure life because we are told to 'put on the Lord Jesus Christ and not to think about how to satisfy the desires of the flesh,' in Romans 13:14. We are also instructed to 'be holy as the Lord is holy,' but the pursuit of purity is not an easy thing to adhere to. In this day and age, it's not easy to avoid the constant barrage of seducing images. From commercials to clothing and everything in between, it seems that sexual messages are constantly playing before our eyes. Media, society and even psychology often justify sexual impropriety. Yet, even psychologists don't seem to know the ramifications and dangers of entertaining and living with these spirits. We live in a day when 'anything goes.'

It's important to recognize several things at work. Lust, pornography, personal sexual gratification, and fantasy are open doors that the enemy uses to entice people through sexual enjoyment. Satan works through romance novels, video games, porn and other graphic things that defile the mind and thought life. Things that contribute to impurity in the eye gate all add to a defiled thought life that is easily led astray by wrong thoughts and fantasies. Our minds act as a big movie screen. What we feed it will play over and over again, leading people into acting on those thoughts and fantasies. That is just a fact. One cannot look at certain things and then have those images just struck from the record, so to speak. It stays in the mind and if it's not innocent, it's not without consequence. If a person looks at pornography, they will think about it. If people read lusty novels that spark certain imaginations as they read, then they are playing that image in the movie screen of their mind. It's the same with violence or other unsavory things. Those things become a magnet to the wrong spirits. Sooner or later, the person will be tempted to act on what they put into their mind because demons will feed them the thoughts they want people to act on.

Demonic spirits observe us all the time. They know our likes and dislikes, and where we have weaknesses. They know how to use just the right bait to entice a person to open a door to them so that they can really get their hooks into a person. Little by little, as a person partakes of certain things, demons feel comfortable in that person's life. The person is deceived into thinking that they are acting on their own free will, but each time they partake of the same sin, they lose their resolve to say no. The demonic presence grows stronger until the person is so chained to the sin, they cannot break free. They have been seduced into shame.

Sometimes these spirits come in through various open doors of abuse (emotional, sexual or physical), molestation, rape, incest or other sexual sins. There can be generational curses that have left an open door to familiar spirits. Lust, witchcraft and other spirits bring defilement and rob people of their purity. Even one sexual partner that has these spirits in their life can transfer them to someone else. That makes a great argument for no premarital sex and saving oneself for marriage! The reality, though, is that there are billions of people on earth that are at the very least curious and interested in sex, pornography, and other things, and they don't wait for marriage. They don't understand this sort of thing. They have opened themselves up to making the enemy quite comfortable to visit them whether or not they think they may have invited him.

There are those that have had things happen to them that they didn't want to occur, such as molestation or abuse, and they are just as troubled. I've known women who were abused and raped. Some were by pimps that were initiating them into the sex trade industry. While this is not true of all people, there are those that become addicted to that lifestyle and don't want out. They feel tied to their abusers and they don't know why. They just keep running back to the lifestyle, or the lifestyle doesn't seem to leave them regardless of whether or not they continue in the industry. It's because of the spiritual ties. If a person cannot seem to stop thinking or desiring someone that is obviously bad for them, they must renounce the soul ties and familiar spirits, the sins of adultery and whoredom, otherwise they can stay chained to spirits that will abuse and accuse them. So many have lost hope because they feel there is no way out for them. These people are living with the feelings of being fearful, dirty, defiled, guilty, angry, afraid and ashamed and don't know what to do about it. They feel defective, as if there is something wrong with them. The truth is, it is not them that is defective. It is the presence of the enemy in their life that has tried to convince them they are someone they are not. There is always hope through Jesus Christ.

One thing that really needs to be stressed is the importance of forgiveness. When a person has suffered at the hands of someone else, through molestation, rape or other sins against their body, they can be linked to those individuals in the spirit. Those unclean spirits that came into their life thorough those sins want to remain. They do manifest as incubus and succubus spirits. What I've noticed is that the person may say, "But I haven't done anything wrong. I don't know why these spirits come on me." Many times that person still has anger or unforgiveness issues to work through towards their abuser. This causes them to have an open door to the enemy, granting him legal right to remain.

I absolutely understand that it is not fair to have to deal

with those spirits that want to molest a person against their will, but the responsibility to forgive the offender still lies with the one who was victimized. God still holds us accountable to His standard. There is a very big difference between just saying the words that you forgive someone, and having those words register as an authentic change of heart. In the parable of the unforgiving servant, Jesus said that the person that did not *forgive from their heart* would be given over to the tormenters until they paid the last cent of what was owed. Some translations omit that part of scripture, which really tends to cause people to miss the entire point of the parable found in Mathew 18:21-35. Let me quote the last couple of verses for you:

"The king turned over the unmerciful slave to his brigade of torturers, and they had their way with him until he should pay his whole debt. And that is what My Father in heaven will do to you, unless you forgive each of your brothers and each of your sisters from the very cockles of your heart." (Matthew 18:34,35 VOICE)

We can see that God's goal is complete and genuine forgiveness. Working through emotional issues can be difficult. Incorporate fasting. It really does help. One thing that perhaps I can help others understand is that the forgiveness isn't so much for the one who offended you as it is for yourself. The one who wronged you is just as accountable to God as you are. No one is getting off the hook easily unless they genuinely repent. God is fair and just. I guarantee you, if there has not been genuine repentance between that person and God, they will suffer for it. Whether or not you ever find out about their personal suffering is irrelevant. If you are waiting for that moment so that you can savor the moment and rejoice in someone else's pain, then that should tell you something about yourself. God is not pleased with that kind of attitude. You can trust God with the situation that wounded you.

Remember what I wrote earlier, about how the enemy worms his way into a person's belief system, and how he perverts the way a person thinks? Sometimes the generational curses and demonic spirits are waiting to go to work on someone from the moment they are born. A child does not have a way to defend themselves from the things that are set against them. That innocent baby grows up into a person with a twisted sense of right and wrong, and sometimes has limited control over their actions because of the demons controlling them. Obviously, it is not an excuse for wrong actions, but it can help us understand that they, too, became a victim of demonic oppression. I pray that this will help others reading this to be able to see the one that hurt them in a different light. You know when forgiveness is genuine because you will feel your heart soften towards the one that hurt you. And *that* is the very thing the enemy does not want to happen, because it closes the door he's used to gain access to a person's life. Then the person can stand upon the scripture in James 4:6,7 and the enemy can't do anything about it. When a person is genuinely submitted to God, then they can resist the enemy and command him to go. That's when you tell all those incubus & succubus spirits, perverse spirits, lust, all of them to get out. Those devils have to obey.

SPIRIT HUSBANDS AND SPIRIT WIVES

When incubus and succubus spirits or other perverse spirits are in a person's life, they assume the role of husband or wife. They become a covenant partner which must be renounced and DIVORCED. They will defile even a Christian marriage through ungodly, impure fantasy, porn and other things. *A demonic spirit of any kind will never be satisfied with something pure or godly. It will come to despise it, because Satan despises God's order.* Any demonic spirit will resist and seek ways to defile what God intends to be pure.

We touched on the fact that sex outside of marriage can invite the wrong spirits into a person's life, and how it can also cause the enemy to become bonded to us. It can become quite a battle to try to shut these spirits down and evict them. Sometimes one partner is the discerner and the one pressing for purity and change, while the other spouse may take longer to come through the process. God uses the prayers of one partner to pull the other one into their freedom, but expect those spirits to push back! They are very jealous for the object of their affections and don't give up easily. One or both partners can experience the voice and influence of demonic suggestions in their thought life. They can hear those voices internally or externally. Spirits frequently talk to us by planting suggestions as if it is our own thought. Example: "This is what I like; I should be able to enjoy myself." "No one else will find out, and I'm not hurting anyone. What's wrong with it?" Or, "I cannot change because I was born this way. This is just what I prefer." Spirits will also speak to a person externally, as a voice projected to us from outside of us. This can come through another person as well as a voice in our ears. Example: "You are boring. You need to be more adventurous." Or, "You are so _____ (Fill in the blank)." It sounds like more of a complaint and feels like an accusation, like you're the problem and not the behavior. More than likely, that is the perverse spirit speaking, along with the spirit of accusation. It wants to pressure people into tolerating it and making an ungodly peace treaty with it. There could be any number of thoughts and suggestions that really don't agree with a sense of purity or our true identity in Christ, but I'll leave it at that. There are a variety of personal opinions and legalistic perspectives from different people, that are not necessarily coming from the word of God. Let the conviction of the Holy Spirit be your guide. When a person is used to listening and agreeing with the wrong spirits for a long time, it can be very difficult to discern that they are not coming from ourselves. Demons will pout, accuse and make their displeasure known. They will use rejection to make the other spouse feel they are not appealing or able to satisfy the other partner. This can cause anger, hurt, strife and separation in the relationship, but this is how the enemy tries to convince the one who is bound that they cannot find sexual fulfillment without that spirit being present. It does not want that person to realize that God's design for marriage does not need help from demons to make it satisfying. It's important to remember that if something feels unclean, don't ignore your conscience. Anything that violates a person's conscience or causes them to feel uncomfortable should be a red flag. Your conscience is there for a reason, to guard you and keep you in the ways of righteousness.

The enemy wants people to maintain a covenant with him. Recognize this is the enemy trying to hold his ground. Forgive one another quickly and realize this is how the enemy plays his game. Pray that the eyes of the affected person, the one who is caught up in putting the wrong things before their eyes, no longer desires the things that are impure. Bind the perverse spirit along with lust and idolatry; release the spirit of conviction, humility, repentance and purity. Only God can set the person free.

One of the key things that Satan takes advantage of is the secrecy involved in these sort of sins. He will help a person rationalize things in order to keep those secrets tucked away in the darkness, and that is where he hides. That is where he manipulates a person's thoughts. Secrecy is where the enemy seeks to unravel the covenant of honesty, the covenant of trust, and the covenant between a husband and wife. It is also how he puts a wedge between the believer and God. **Anytime we try to protect or preserve an area of our heart and life that is not submitted to God, it places us in relationship with the enemy.** This can be seen in the spirit realm as making a covenant with darkness and can be thought of as a form of spiritual adultery. We can only be loyal to one, and we must choose where we place our loyalties. If the enemy is working on helping people keep a secret, then he is working on lies, because self-deception and lies begin in our own heart. Then they are told to others as a means of defending the stronghold and the behavior he wants us to protect. When the enemy looks for an inroad, he is looking for ways to produce a domino effect. All he needs is to set off one that will trigger a chain reaction and cause much more trouble and heartache. When the covenant of trust and respect are undermined, the foundation of that relationship is broken and it's very difficult to get that back.

When one spouse turns to fantasizing about someone other than their partner it is a form of rejection. There is an area where it feels like trust has been broken. For some, it can feel like betrayal and sometimes just as painful as if the person had an affair. They rejected the person they were supposed to turn to for intimacy, and chose a counterfeit instead. In many cases, that can feel a lot like unfaithfulness. In Matthew 5:28 Jesus said,

"But I say, anyone who even looks at a woman with lust has already committed adultery with her in his heart."

Some people might argue with that line of thinking. They might say that thinking about something is not the same as acting upon it. However, Jesus said something similar in a another portion of scripture, and so did the Apostle John.

Jesus said, *"But the things that come out of your mouth—your curses, your fears, your denunciations—these come from your heart, and it is the stirrings of your heart that can make you unclean. For your heart harbors evil thoughts—fantasies of murder, adultery, and whoring; fantasies of stealing, lying, and slandering."* (Matt.15:18,19)

In 1 John 3:15, Apostle John also drew the connection between the thought life and a subsequent action.

"Anyone who hates another brother or sister is really a murderer at heart. And you know that murderers don't have eternal life within them." (1 John 3:15 NLT)

What was really in question was who the person identified with: God, or Satan. What qualities are most like God, and which are most like Satan? Jesus was looking at the intent of the heart, and He was quick to connect the dots between a thought birthing a subsequent, related action. Satan plants seeds in the soil of our thought life. If we are not quick to cast down those vain imaginations, those seeds will come to rest in the soil of our heart. Every seed produces after its kind. Eventually the seed will bear fruit and an action will be born. Lust is the seed of adultery just as much as hatred is the seed of murder.

Inviting another partner into the marriage, even if it is through fantasy, porn or adultery is no small matter. Not only does it affect the feelings of the other spouse, but it also serves as an invitation for the perverse spirit to participate in that marriage. That spirit becomes their covenant partner until both agree to renounce it and divorce the enemy. If there are children in the family, what is invited into the lives of the couple also affects them. It's unavoidable.

Broken covenants and broken vows can occur when the trust in a relationship has been damaged. This becomes an open door for a curse to come in until the person confesses that sin. It doesn't have to be a physical affair, although if adulterous thoughts are entertained long enough, it will eventually lead to that. Satan never wants people to consider where his temptations and lies will lead them. Satan's first course of action is not usually temptation, it is tiredness. He works to wear a person down. I've known of women who nagged their husbands incessantly, used the silent treatment, guilt and rejection, even withheld sex from their husbands – some for a year or longer - then blamed their husbands when they sought love elsewhere. The Bible issues a warning against such behavior, saying that our bodies no longer belong just to us, but to one another. If we deprive one another of sexual intimacy for an extended period of time, that can very well give the enemy opportunity to bring in the wrong sort of temptation.[44] Obviously there will

---

[44] 1 Cor. 7:3-5

always be situations where people may need to work through them, but the issue is to *work through them*, not resort to punishing one another. Spouses that refuse to forgive, harbor offense and take on a bitter spirit will repel their mates. If a spouse refuses to change so that they fulfil the needs of their mate, then the enemy will succeed in gaining a foothold in that marriage. Marriage is about love, respect and nurturing one another. When one partner is hurting, it affects everyone in the house. Don't settle for living with wounds; make the right decision to do what is necessary to get healthy. It closes the door to the enemy and your family will thank you for it.

Another type of opportunity the enemy looks for are those in ministry. There have been pastors who were so overworked and distracted that they failed to discern when they should have left the door open to their counseling sessions or kept more of a distance with other women. One thing can lead to another, and they can form bonds with someone other than their spouse. Seducing spirits strategize with one another, and look for opportunities to bring temptation. People tend to forget that pastors are but men, and they are just as prone to slipping into temptation as anyone else. In fact, the enemy works doubly hard on those in ministry in an attempt to *make* them fall. That's not an excuse for the wrong behavior, but all people are created with certain human needs. The enemy we fail to discern is the one who might get one over on us. He is always seeking an opportunity.

A person that is tired, overworked or distracted, is more likely to be careless and let their guard down. It's the person who gets too close to a co-worker, or the person who feels neglected at home that often turns to someone or something outside the marriage for comfort. Typically, men have a higher statistic for getting involved in porn more so than women. They do not stop to think about how damaging it is to a marriage. I have counseled other women, including pastor's wives, that felt terribly hurt and betrayed by their husband's actions. Above all perhaps, is the fact that it creates a mess of emotional responses: jealousy, suspicion, inferiority, insecurity, anger, and feelings of rejection. It destroys intimacy and communication, not to mention the loss of respect that their spouse must then work to earn back. When trust is broken, it isn't automatically restored. It takes humility, time and effort to rebuild the foundation of trust. Many people find themselves slowly going down that road, not with the intention to have an affair, but the effect is just as damaging.

The enemy will make sure that the sin is discovered, because that was his intent from the beginning. Satan's goal is to break the foundation of trust. People only tend to think about the temptation, or the excitement of how they feel at the moment, without considering that the enemy has already planned out his desired end. He knows exactly how to lay down the bait to lure his victim into the trap. With that in mind, people must ask themselves if it is worth it to risk breaking the foundational covenant in their marriage. *Ignore the seduction of the siren's call. It will pull you into deep water and drown you.*

THE PERVERSE SPIRIT

A perverse spirit turns things upside down. What is forbidden by God begins to sound appealing. What is pure and right, is considered undesirable, void of any satisfaction, or insufficient. **The enemy's strategy is not always straightforward, but it is always strategic**. When he wants to seduce someone away from God's order for sexual fulfillment, he has to first destroy the conscience.

God has instilled a conscience into every human being, because it gives people an innate sense of right or wrong. Because we are made in the image of God, this moral compass is there to help keep people in the ways of God. A person's conscience will either accuse or acquit us on the day we stand before Him, to have our lives reviewed in the final judgement. [45]

Satan knows that the conscience will feel guilt when that moral standard is violated. If the person is a Christian, they will be prompted to confess their sin. Obviously, the enemy doesn't want that, so he finds ways to slowly turn off the conscience. The work of the perverse spirit is to find ways to introduce a new set of standards that the person will justify and defend. Before he can do that, he must first create soul wounds. The enemy methodically and repeatedly counters the natural desire God instilled in them with tactics that will cause that person to want to reject what is good in God's eyes. It doesn't always have to take on the idea of being bad, just *undesirable*; therefore what is pure and right as God's plan for emotional and sexual fulfillment is rejected in favor of something else. This can be between a husband and a wife, or it can occur in those who eventually turn to embrace porn, adultery, or same-sex relationships. The thing to understand is that the enemy looks for ways to make a person disappointed or dissatisfied so they will embrace a forbidden desire. In order to turn a person to reject God's ordained order for relationships, the stage must first be set for a person to become disappointed or dissatisfied with His will.

---

[45] Romans 2:14-16.

For instance, in situations before a person turns to the gay or homosexual lifestyle, they may encounter repeated disappointment and rejection of certain male/female relationships. The enemy does this to turn them away from God's natural order so that they will seek comfort in an alternative lifestyle. Disappointment turns to a loss of hope, then a fear that either they are unlovable or unable to find acceptance and love with the opposite sex. This fear turns to a rejection of truth, feelings of anger, and many times, bitterness. When the enemy feels the person has been sufficiently prepared to embrace a counterfeit to God's plan, he introduces someone of the same sex. Usually by then the person is so desperate for a sense of love, comfort and acceptance that they will not reject the illegitimate means of comfort and love. Conviction is ignored and repeatedly shunned; to acknowledge conviction would mean having to also acknowledge accountability to God. *Bingo.* The conscience is turned off and truth is rejected. Do you see the perverse spirit at work? What follows next is an increased deterioration of moral standards into depravity. There is a warning about rejecting God and rejecting truth. It is found in Romans chapter one.

"For I am not the least bit embarrassed about the gospel. I won't shy away from it, because it is God's power to save every person who believes: first the Jew, and then the non-

Jew. You see, in the good news, God's restorative justice is revealed. And as we will see, it begins with and ends in faith. As the Scripture declares, "By faith the just will obtain life."

"For the wrath of God is breaking through from heaven, opposing all manifestations of ungodliness and wickedness by the people who do wrong to keep God's truth in check. These people are not ignorant about what can be known of God, because He has shown it to them with great clarity. From the beginning, creation in its magnificence enlightens us to His nature. Creation itself makes His undying power and divine identity clear, even though they are invisible; and it voids the excuses and ignorant claims of these people because, despite the fact that they knew the one true God, they have failed to show the love, honor, and appreciation due to the One who created them! Instead, their lives are consumed by vain thoughts that poison their foolish hearts. They claim to be wise; but they have been exposed as fools, frauds, and con artists— only a fool would trade the splendor and beauty of the immortal God to worship images of the common man or woman, bird or reptile, or the next beast that tromps along."

*"So God gave them just what their **lustful** hearts desired. As a result, they violated their bodies and **invited shame** into their lives. How? By choosing a foolish lie over*

God's truth." (Rom. 1:16-25 VOICE)

Reflect back for a moment to what I wrote earlier on Lilith, (incubus and succubus spirits). It is said that incubus and succubus spirits are the same spirit, but able to switch between male or female, so they have bisexual abilities and possess the power to influence others in a similar fashion. It is easy to see how these demonic spirits can cause confusion over gender identity and sexual orientation issues, and also be recognized as a root cause of homosexuality. When truth is rejected, the person will automatically embrace the lie; and, with the lie, Satan is then able to change a person's identity to reflect his image of perversion.

Familiar spirits can be a part of someone's life from the moment they are born. That is why people can swear up and down they were 'born gay' or born with certain other preferences when in fact it is actually caused by demonic spirits. Sometimes people that are struggling with gender confusion or conflicting thoughts about sexual identity have actually been influenced to believe a lie spoken by other individuals close to them. A comment such as, "You're just like me," spoken by a person that identifies with the gay lifestyle, or a statement such as, "Your parents always wanted a boy," can actually serve to convince a person of a lie. When someone agrees with a lying spirit, it allows demonic spirits to attach to them. The enemy can then influence them to become someone that God never intended.

After a time of rejecting God's attempt to convict a person to turn away from sin, and they continuously reject Him, their heart becomes increasingly resistant to truth. They no longer sense a desire to repent. When a person continually rejects the Holy Spirit, that person's heart becomes hardened in their sin. It becomes very, very difficult for people to come back from a heart that can no longer acknowledge a need for repentance. A person with a hardened heart that refuses to repent will eventually suffer the consequences of their actions, because God lifts His hand of protection from them.

There are familiar spirits that remain in families to reproduce certain sins and lifestyles. It may skip a generation or two, then reappear, which is why it can sometimes not be considered as a generational curse. Also, in households where the female is controlling, abusive and male leadership is greatly lacking or subdued by a dominant female, there will be greater instances of children turning to the gay or perverse lifestyle. This occurs because the order is upside down. It's reversed. God has chosen the male authority to be dominant over the family unit, not the female. God has chosen the male authority to represent Christ to the family. The male authority is designed by God to protect, cover, instruct, and discipline the household in righteousness so that good fruit and godly offspring are the result of a divinely ordered union between a man and a woman. This is God's order.

It is not loving or kind to allow anyone to fool themselves into thinking that people can sin with impunity. We are all held accountable to the truth. Truth is not based on feelings or opinions, but on the word of God. Truth is also the person of the Holy Spirit. There is a holy, loving God that has made a provision for our sin, and that is the blood sacrifice of Jesus Christ. All we have to do is accept His provision! Trying to deny or avoid truth does not lessen the penalties for breaking God's laws.

1 Corinthians 6:9-10 says,

"Or do you not know that the unrighteous will not inherit the kingdom of God? Do not be deceived; neither fornicators, nor idolaters, nor adulterers, nor effeminate, nor homosexuals, nor thieves, nor the covetous, nor drunkards, nor revilers, nor swindlers, will inherit the kingdom of God...."

And, Galatians 5:20,21 says this:

"...idolatry, sorcery, enmities, strife, jealousy, outbursts of anger, disputes, dissensions, factions, envying, drunkenness, carousing, and things like these, of which I forewarn you, just as I have forewarned you, that those who practice such things will not inherit the kingdom of God."

You must walk in the truth that you know, for the truth that you know is how you will be judged by God.

Father,

Help me to stop defending what you call sin. You can't heal what I attempt to hide, defend and protect. Give me the conviction to go to war against these wrong beliefs and the spirits associated with them instead of making peace treaties. Help me to drive the enemy out so that I can live in freedom and victory. In Jesus name, amen.

CHAPTER 7
RENOUNCING OLD COVENANTS

The word covenant is not a word I find to be common language, except when one is specifically referring to scriptures. In a dream I heard the Lord say, "Renounce old covenants!"

I know that God was not referring to every covenant, but He was clear about His intent. He mentioned specifically covenants of regret. A covenant is a contract. He wants His people to renounce the agreements we have unknowingly had with the enemy. The word covenant can obviously be applied in a positive manner, such as a marriage covenant or the way God has chosen to honor His covenant with us. In a marriage, there is a promise and an intent of two parties in mutual agreement to live with one another and share in the stipulations of that contract that both parties agree upon. Even business contracts are often similar in nature. However, in this context the word covenant has a negative connotation. It refers to an agreement or a contract between two parties that is legally binding. Remember, Satan is a legalist. Every devil, including Satan himself, examines us for the legal right to enforce the negative consequences of our actions.

Dictionary.com offers several definitions of the word.

Covenant:

1. An agreement, usually formal, between two or more persons to do or not do something specified.

2. Law. an incidental clause in such an agreement.

3. In relationship to law, a covenant is a formal agreement of legal validity, especially one under seal.

It also means a promise to enter into a covenant between two people or parties, a pledge.

In my dream, the Lord brought several people to pray for me and they told me to break the old covenant I had with regret. I said I didn't know I had made a covenant with regret, but the person in my dream said, "It doesn't matter if you did it knowingly or unknowingly, you still need to renounce it because the enemy is enforcing it!"

We all have blind spots, and I think that was the point the Lord wanted to impress upon me. The enemy hides from us, so it's the Lord's job to drive him out of hiding. That's why we will experience certain areas of our lives where it seems like we can't seem to get the victory for the longest time. God shows us the problem often by making us miserable with our own frustrations and limitations. Then when we get around to asking the right question, He will come with the revelation that helps us understand how to get free.

The enemy hides from us, but there are still tell-tale signs that he is at work. Our triggers, frustrations, and emotional struggles can help us pinpoint what enemy needs to be evicted. Past and Regret are demons assigned to keep people chained to their past. Shame is another one. They must be renounced. If you are curious as to why I frequently use that word, it is because it is synonymous with the word 'divorce.' You must state your intent to enforce your will and disavow yourself from the enemy. You are making the statement that do not wish to be yoked to him and you are commanding him to leave!

Although the enemy tries to stay hidden, God will send conflicts, emotional responses, the recollection of certain memories and other things that serve to flush the enemy out of hiding so that we will not be able to ignore the struggle. These things serve to sting the conscience whereby we experience a certain amount of discomfort and pain, because those are the things that provoke people to ask the right questions. Negative memories serve two purposes. The enemy uses them to remind us who we used to be, and God uses them to uncover the works of evil. Do you ever have some negative memory pop up out of nowhere? Many times that will be the enemy trying to pull a person back under guilt, shame, anger or some other unhealthy feeling. Next time that happens, ask Holy Spirit to show you His perspective on that situation. Ask Him to show you something that will heal that memory and give you the ability to see yourself in a different light. God uses hidden things to bring them up to the surface where He can deal with it.

"Moreover, the LORD your God will send hornets among them, until those who are left and hide themselves from you are destroyed." (Deut. 7:20)

This is one of the ways that God leads us out of old behavior and into our true identity in Christ. The things that God drives out are the enemies of our soul. They keep people wounded, distrustful, insecure and in captivity to many other negative emotions. Those things separate us from being able to live as new creations in Christ. The new version of who we are is much better!

Jesus told his disciples that if they continued in His word they would be His disciples, but on their part they would have to learn how to resist evil, obey His commands and trust Him. In doing these things, they would come to understand His teaching, be led by His Spirit, and also learn where their hope and trust were truly anchored – in Him. Jesus' response is this:

"Then you will know the truth, and the truth will set you free." (John 8:32)

GETTING DELIVERED

Sex addiction is a real problem for many people. Obviously there are a wide range of physiological and genetic differences in every person that contribute to the libido and natural desires. Some people may have more difficulty controlling their cravings than others, but a person that struggles with addiction will never know what 'normal' really is unless they receive healing from their soul wounds and receive deliverance from demonic attachments.

The spirits that have been discussed are predator spirits.

Lust, incubus, succubus and other perverse spirits are the cause of many sins, much shame and fear. These spirits are responsible for molestation and abuse of their victims. When I use the term 'molestation,' it can be by a demonic spirit alone, or using someone else as its host in order to inflict torment and bondage upon a person. Either way, an evil spirit is involved. It just doesn't always have a physical form or a host body.

These same spirits are also responsible for crimes involving molestation, pedophilia, rape, incest and sexual abuse. Regardless of whether a person is the perpetrator or the victim, they need healing and deliverance. Rape, molestation and sexual abuse are very traumatic events that leave the victims with painful memories. It can also leave them with demonic attachments that came from their abuser. These spirits are fear, anger, shame, insecurity, distrust, unforgiveness and bitterness, as well as incubus or succubus, lust, incest, the perverse spirit or more. When the trauma is very severe, it can also cause depression, confusion, perversion, insanity, sickness and death. Once the door has been opened to the enemy, it is anyone's guess how Satan will decide to use other spirits in his plan to cause further pain and torment.

Victims should have counseling to help process the

emotional trauma, but they should also have prayer counseling by someone that can offer compassionate healing ministry. Without it they cannot get free from the demonic attachments that will continue to torment them. Through the power of prayer, we can deal with issues that have left a person with deep emotional pain, shame and a whole host of other things. The only time people cannot be set free is when they are somehow in agreement with a sinful attitude or unwilling to part with sin. Evil spirits will not leave if their host is in agreement with them. One of the biggest lies people tell themselves is that they are 'ok' when all they've really done is swept those painful events under the carpet. Some are buried so deep people are no longer aware that they need healing. Their own heart has deceived them. But, if they were to ask God for His perspective, He would show them a radically different picture. Just because someone is out of touch with their feelings doesn't mean they are healed! God loves us so much that He refuses to let the pain remain buried. He knows that if He left people in that condition then all that toxic waste would eventually destroy their lives. If you are in pain, bondage or at a crossroads, I encourage you to bring your problems to Jesus and let Him heal you. Today is a day for a fresh start!

Father God,

I need a Savior, a Deliverer. Lord Jesus, I believe you paid the price for my sin and shame when you went to the cross on my behalf. I do not have to bear the weight of it any longer. Jesus, I pray that Your blood would wash over my mind, my body and my spirit and make me clean. Renew in me a pure thought life.

I come to you to ask you for cleansing from any unclean spirits. I take responsibility for the things I've done, the things I've allowed, and even things that have been done to me against my will. Right now I forgive _____ (speak the names of those that have sinned against you) so that I can also have my own sins forgiven, and I ask You to empower me to do so. As a matter of my will, I choose to forgive them and ask that You, Father, give me grace and strength to not take any offense back into my heart. I ask that You heal those that have perpetrated sins against me, and set us free from the spirits that has had us bound.

Lord Jesus, I give myself to You and ask that You forgive my sin. Please forgive me as well as the sins of my ancestors. Forgive all the ways that we rejected You and rebelled against your ways, and exerted our independence from You. Forgive idolatry, rebellion, witchcraft, involvement with the occult, shedding innocent blood, broken vows and covenants. Forgive the many things we have done to deny Your Lordship. Let Your blood cover our sins, I pray. Be Lord of my life. I take You as my Savior, Master, Husband, Friend, and Lord. I will not have any other gods besides You. I make a covenant with You, Jesus. Help me to be faithful to You. Thank you, Father, for accepting me and adopting me into the kingdom of God.

Satan, I divorce you. You are not my husband or my master. I renounce all covenants with spirits known as Past, Regret, and Shame. I renounce every demonic spirit that has been a part of my life. I want nothing to do with you ever again. I reject your seed and your lies. I reject, refuse, renounce and divorce all unclean demonic spirits of lust, perversity including incubus, mare and succubus spirits, pornography, pedophilia, voyeurism, domination, brutality, homosexuality, confusion, gender confusion, astral projection and spirit travel, double-mindedness, unbelief, sodomy, rape, incest, anger, rage, guilt, rejection, bitterness, unforgiveness, witchcraft, idolatry, hardheartedness, accusation, familiar and familial spirits, pride, rebellion, and death. I renounce and divorce Lilu, Lilith, and all lillin spirits, those known as Lamia and vampire spirits, and all that comes from Satan and his demons. I repent for any ways that I have knowingly or unknowingly come into agreement with these spirits, and I humbly submit myself to the Lord Jesus Christ and the authority of His Holy Spirit.

I submit to You, O God, and I resist the enemy, commanding him to flee from me and take everything he has put on me, everything he has brought into my life, and every seed that he has implanted into my belief system. I curse Satan's seed and declare, "YOU WILL BEAR NO MORE FRUIT EVER AGAIN," by the name and authority of Jesus Christ. His blood covers these sins and I command these doors to be shut, never to open again.

Let every cord of sin, shame, fear, witchcraft, and soul ties from ungodly sources be severed now, in Jesus name. I renounce the soul ties to former lovers, spouses, authority figures and others that may be tied to me in the spirit. Let any fragments of their souls return to them, and let any scattered and fragmented parts of my soul return to me, in Jesus name. Let all those that would practice astral projection, spirit travel, witchcraft or other occult practices against me find the door closed. Let there be blindness into this evil eye now. I bind and forbid the entrance or demonic spirits into my life in Jesus name, according to your promise in Matthew 18:18. What is bound on earth has already been bound in heaven.

I loose myself from all shame, resentment, fear, trauma, bitterness, anger, rage, insecurity and feelings of inferiority that have come upon me as a result of sexual molestation and other sins against my body - both those that were done without my consent, and those that I may have participated in - willingly or unwillingly. I renounce all generational rebellion, false gods, and the covenants that have been made with these demonic entities by myself or my ancestors. I renounce and forsake all New Age practices, the false gods associated with other religions, including Buddhism, Hinduism, The Illuminati, occult practices, yoga, the Kundalini and serpent spirits. I renounce all alternative forms of medicine, Ayurveda and acupuncture that have opened a door to the enemy. I command all spirits associated with these practices to go back to the abyss in Jesus name. I bind the screech owl that brings terror by night and forbid it to enter my life, that of my family or my home, in the name and authority of Jesus Christ.

I submit to You, O God, and I resist the enemy, commanding him to flee from me and take everything he has put on me, everything he has brought into my life, and every seed that he has implanted into my belief system and go now. I command all evil trees, ungodly seeds and demonic roots to come out, shrivel and die immediately, in Jesus name. Let all evil trees be pulled up by the roots out of my life now in Jesus name. Let every ungodly altar be dismantled. I command every spirit that does not worship Jesus Christ; every spirit that does not confess Jesus Christ has come in the flesh, and any spirit that does not declare Jesus Christ as its Lord and Master to leave me and my household at once, in the name of Jesus.

I receive by faith the healing for my mind, my emotions, my body and spirit. I receive by faith the mind of Christ, and I choose this day to pull up the root of bitterness and replace it with the love of God. I ask You Lord to plant forgiveness, purity, obedience, peace, joy and love in my heart and life. Fill me with Your Holy Spirit and let the spirit of adoption be poured out into my heart in Jesus name. Let your love and acceptance captivate my heart, O God.

I receive by faith healing for my emotions, belief system, and perspective towards God, myself and others. I declare: "Because the Great I AM lives within me, I become what YOU are, O God. Because the living word of God dwells within me; You are transforming me, renewing my mind, to become the living word, as Your truth is lived out in me. You are transforming me to become the anointed of God. I am not a victim, I am victorious! I do not fear; the enemy is fearful of me! I declare that no weapon formed against me shall prosper, and every tongue that rises up against me is refuted according to Your word in Isaiah 54:17. I walk in the fullness of God, in Jesus name.

I thank you, Lord Jesus, for being my healer, restorer, redeemer and protector. I thank you for replacing every lie in my belief system with the truth that will set me free. Thank You, Holy Spirit for releasing revelation as to my true identity in Christ. Show me how You see me. Show me where I have believed lies about my true identity. I thank You for establishing and settling me in faith and truth.

Help me, Lord Jesus, to identify and break free from any relationships that are unhealthy and undesirable in Your eyes. Help me to honor Your word, Your will and Your wishes. You know my weaknesses; I pray for strength to overcome them. For those things that You know I cannot or will not be able to overcome in my own strength, I pray that You would take them out of my hand. Let it be done according to Your will for my life and for the benefit of Your will carried out in the lives of others, too. Lord, replace those relationships with better ones that will strengthen me in my walk with you, and fill the void for love, relationship and friendship.

Father God, I thank You for overcoming victory. Please fill me with Your Holy Spirit and empower me to live for You.

Help me to live a life that honors You and brings You glory. In Jesus name, Amen.

CHAPTER 8
LIVING IN A NEW IDENTITY

Pastor Bill Burkhardt is a trusted friend, a caring and compassionate pastor, and he also carries a powerful prophetic mantle. His insights on the subject of identity have been a tremendous revelation and blessing to the body of Christ. He experienced the frustration of feeling inadequate to please those he loved, unsure about his identity, and lived with feelings of shame and rejection. What I admire about Bill is the fact that he allows himself to be vulnerable in sharing his experiences with transformation. God has given him one of the most insightful and refreshing teachings on identity that I've ever had the pleasure of listening to, and I have asked him to share his thoughts. The rest of this chapter is in his words.

I grew up in a household of perfectionism. My parents had little ability to love me unconditionally because they had never received unconditional love from their parents. Approval was achieved through performance, and I could never do anything well enough to feel approved of by my parents. My parents did their best to love me, but I often felt like a nuisance to them and that they merely tolerated me. I can't remember feeling enjoyed by my parents.

When I came to Christ more than 3 decades ago, I was taught that Jesus loved me. I thought I believed that Jesus loved me, but in reality I had little ability to receive God's love. For the first several decades of my Christian life, my experience with God's love was mostly intellectual.

My childhood experience locked me into a subconscious belief that something was deeply wrong with me. I still believed what I learned as a child - that I couldn't ever do anything well enough to be approved of. I believed that if someone got to know me well enough, they would eventually discover I was unlovable.

About a decade ago, God began to help me discover that He not only loves me, He *enjoys* me. God was so determined to reveal His enjoyment of me that this truth has been transforming my heart and has become the signature message of my life.

What really happened was God broke the shame-based identity from my heart, and replaced it with a new identity rooted in the love of God. I discovered that I didn't have to be loveable to qualify for God's love. God loves me because He wants to. I began to actually experience being loved and enjoyed by God, rather than merely mentally assenting to that truth. I began to experience God's love and this experience empowered to love Him back. God helped me to love God!

This journey into discovering God's love began with listening to a Mike Bickle series on Song of Solomon. The Holy Spirit emphasized the theme of the Father's enjoyment of me. I began to see it everywhere in Scripture. The truth that God enjoys me renewed my mind and transformed my life.

The transformation of your identity based on the love of God is what I want for you! Life is too valuable for you to plod along with a shame-based identity when God wants you to enjoy life.

God wants to radically and supernaturally equip you to receive His love in a way that enables you to radically and supernaturally love Him back. It is the Lord Himself that has the power to equip you to obey his simplified commandments to love God and love people.

In fact, the "joy of the Lord is your strength" (Neh. 8:10). That means His joy for you gives you strength. The source of your strength depends on your ability to receive the Lord's enjoyment of you. In a healthy family, children are enjoyed by their parents. As a child of God, you have been invited into the healthiest family that has ever existed.

The Godhead: Heaven's Prototype Healthy Family

As part of Jesus' prayer to the Father before he goes to the cross, Jesus refers to the glory that exists in the Godhead:

"In this moment, Father, fuse Our collective glory and bring Us together as We were before creation existed."
John 17:5 (The Voice version)

There is a "collective glory" that radiates from the relationship between God the Father and God the Son. This glory has existed from before creation. The Father-Son relationship in heaven is full of love and honor. The mutual enjoyment between Father and Son is so intense that the relational bliss can only be described as glory!

There is another Bible passage that provides a unique glimpse of the Father-Son relationship in heaven. The passage in Proverbs 8:22-31 describe a partnership between God the Father and God the Son in the process of creation. Jesus is referred to as "Wisdom" in Proverbs 8:1. "Wisdom" was at His Father's side in creation's workshop:

Creation's Workshop

"Then I (Jesus) was beside Him as a master craftsman;" (Proverbs 8:30a)

When Jesus became a man, his vocation was carpenter. In heavens workshop during the process of creation, He is a "master craftsman." God the Father is functioning as designer-architect, and God the Son is functioning as a master builder. Father and Son are partners in the process of creation. The Father dreams up a design, and the Son is the master craftsman that implements His Father's design.

During this creative process the interaction between Father and Son is full of joy. Mutual enjoyment between Father and Son seem to be an integral part of the creative process. The words "delight" and "rejoicing" are used several times in Proverbs 8:30-31. Jesus says,

"I was daily His (the Fathers') delight, rejoicing always before Him." (Proverbs 8:30b)

Jesus was the focal point of the His Father's joy and delight.   The Father greatly enjoys this creative partnership with His Son. When the Father looks at His son, His face beams with delight! Every day, Jesus experiences the radiant joy beaming from His Fathers' face, and He absorbs His Father's joy. Daily, Jesus becomes so full of His Father's delight that He can't contain the all the joy.   So Jesus expresses His joy by rejoicing!

The process of creation is most certainly an ambitious project. The Father and Son create a universe that is full of divine order and aesthetic beauty.   Their intricate design, attention to detail and masterful craftsmanship would seem to require a focused, serious attitude. But instead, the Bible records a scene that looks more like a party than a job site. Somehow, in the midst of all this delighting and rejoicing, some amazing work gets accomplished.

Not only is Jesus rejoicing because of the Father's delight for Him, He is rejoicing because He is excited about His beautiful finished work of creation.   Jesus rejoices because creation looks so awesome and functions so well.

"Rejoicing in His inhabited world, and my delight was with the sons of men." (Proverbs 8:31)

God Created You because He Enjoys You

Jesus rejoices in His "inhabited world", but then He focuses His delight on mankind:

"My delight was with the sons of men." (Proverbs 8:31)

All the joy that has been streaming from the Father toward Jesus is now streaming from Jesus to you and I! Mankind becomes the focal point of Jesus' joy.

God crafted us so we could experience His joy for us. So you and I are designed to be *enjoyed* by God! The bliss in heavens most healthy family could not be contained. The mutual joy in the Godhead was too good to keep to themselves. You and I were created so God could invite us to into His joyful family! We've been invited to the party!

When a healthy married couple wants a child, the child is conceived because the husband and wife experience joy for one another that cannot be contained. The family is enlarged because husband and wife want to share their joy with someone made in their image. Their child becomes the focal point of their parents joy. This healthy human family is a perfect illustration of why God created you!

God considers you infinitely valuable and He enjoys you and takes great delight in you! As you begin to realize how God see's you, any false identity based on shame dissolves. The revelation of your true identity displaces your inferior identity and transforms your heart.

God Redeemed You because He Enjoys You

God created you because He enjoys you and He will not easily give up this source of His joy in the event you were taken from Him. The Gospel from man's perspective is good news. Jesus restores our relationship with God by His work on the cross.

But the Gospel from God's perspective is equally magnificent. God is not willing to forever forfeit relationship with the one's He has enjoyed from the beginning. He is simply not willing to be left forever without the ones He enjoys. If anything happens that threatens to block relationship with you He is determined to remove the barrier no matter what it costs Him.

The entire Bible can be viewed in three parts:

- God is a Father who wanted a family (Genesis 1-2)
- God lost His kids (Genesis 3)
- God wants His kids back (Genesis 3-Revelation 22)

In Genesis 3, while Adam is hiding from God and attempting to cover his sin, God is coming toward Adam with a plan already in place to restore relationship! God wants His kids back!

God is a Father who loves His kids so much that if one of us gets kidnapped, He will do everything in His power to get us back. Most parents would be willing to lose their life if that's what it took to find and rescue a kidnapped child. The parents of a kidnapped child are tormented day and night until the child is found. There is much rejoicing when a kidnapped child is found safe, rescued and returned to his parents.

The recovery of a lost child and the subsequent rejoicing when the child is found is exactly the subject of Luke chapter 15. The father in Luke 15 can't wait to rejoice when his lost son is found.

God is not aloof, bored or detached when He considers relationship with you. He is not content to sit around in a comfortable house, indifferent to your return. Jesus left heavens comfort zone with one passionate, determined mission: to rescue lots "sons". He considered you and I so valuable that He chose to die rather than live without us!

On the way to the cross, even though He was enduring massive mistreatment and dishonor, He focused instead on "the joy that was set before Him," (Hebrews 12:2) which is you and I! God redeemed you because He enjoys you!

In Luke 15, the Lord is diligently pursuing lost coins, and lost sheep and He passionately rejoices when they are found. He is looking out the window everyday longing for the return of His prodigal son and then sprinting towards him to embrace him!

The story of the prodigal son in Luke 15 is the story of an enormously benevolent, forgiving father. After the prodigal son left home to pursue fulfillment, his father could not stop thinking about the joy and anticipation of his son's return. He would let his son follow his longings, but never lose his desire for restored relationship.

The father never loses the sense of his son's value even though the son was busy displaying uniformly bad behavior. The joy the father has felt for his son since the day he was born is somehow undiminished by his son's poor choices.

As the prodigal son sheepishly returns home, full of shame, he is anticipating a less than joyful reception. He has dishonored his father, lost all his money, pursued self-indulgence, and ended up in the pigpen.

The prodigal son develops a "repentance speech" hoping the father will accept him back as a servant, because he believes his shameful behavior has disqualified him from the privilege of being a son.

He is surprised at the sight of his father running toward him. The father can't contain his joy at his boy's return! The father can't contain his joy at his boy's return! He envelops him in a bear hug even though he must have still reeked with the stench of the pigpen.

The father doesn't make a single reference to the son's bad behavior, and doesn't even let his boy complete his repentance speech. The father is focused only on restoring his son's dignity and all the privileges of being a son. The father's "best robe" over the pig-stained clothing is an exchange for the son's shame for the father's dignity.

This is a picture of the "robe of righteousness God gives us in exchange for our filthy rags." Isaiah 61:10, 64:6. The father's ring on the son's hand is an emblem of fully restored family authority. The sandals provide a "new" source of protection for the son's walk and a renewed sense of purpose for the son's life that is far more noble and respectable than his previous pursuit of self-indulgence. His father can't contain his joy, so he spares no expense in planning for an extravagant party to celebrate his son's return.

If you survey the entire chapter of Luke 15, a distinct theme emerges about our heavenly Father's heart: He likes to celebrate when lost things are recovered and He can't contain his joy when relationship with lost sons is restored. Eleven times in Luke 15 the action of rejoicing is mentioned.

"What man of you, having an hundred sheep, if he lose one of them, doth not leave the ninety and nine in the wilderness, and go after that which is lost, until he find it?

"And when he has found it, he lays it on his shoulders, rejoicing. And when he cometh home, he calls together his friends and neighbors, saying unto them, Rejoice with me; for I have found my sheep which was lost." (Luke 15:4-6)

"Either what woman having ten pieces of silver, if she lose one piece, doth not light a candle, and sweep the house, and seek diligently till she find it?

And when she hath found it, she calls her friends and her neighbors together, saying, Rejoice with me; for I have found the coin that I had lost. Likewise, I say unto you, there is joy in the presence of the angels of God over one sinner that repents." (Luke 15:8-10)

"But the father said to his servants, bring the best robe, and put it on him; and put a ring on his hand, and shoes on his feet: And bring the fatted calf, and kill it; and let us eat, and be merry: For this my son was dead, and is alive again; he was lost, and is found. And they began to be merry." (Luke 15; 22-24)

God is an enormously benevolent, forgiving Father who diligently searches for "lost sons" so He can throw a party in heaven to celebrate restored relationship. The party in Luke 15 is a reflection of the party described in Proverbs 8:30-31. Heaven couldn't contain their joy so the Godhead created man and invited us to join His blissful family. The Godhead created us so we could experience Gods' delight for us and join in on the rejoicing! The Godhead is equally motivated to rejoice when a "lost son" is restored to relationship with God. In fact, all of heaven rejoices when a lost son is restored to the Father (Luke 15:4-7,10).

God so values relationship with each person that He

views people in their unredeemed state as an infinitely valuable lost son. He wants to pursue us and embrace us rather than treat us as a disgusting sinner to avoid.

The Lord places such high value on you He has provided an effective remedy for sin. The death and resurrection of Jesus completely restores your relationship with God (if you accept His gift). Since His remedy for sin is so effective, He is determined to pursue and embrace you rather than reject and avoid you.

Knowing that we have the full assurance of God's love and acceptance - *just the way we are* - opens the door for restored relationship. Those who are disconnected from God are dear to His heart. Everything that Jesus modeled in the gospels was to give mankind a demonstration of divine love. It's the kindness of God that leads men to repentance, and it's His love that leads us home.

CHAPTER 9
GETTING FREE

Demonic spirits feel welcome when they've been a part of a person's life for a long time. They don't want to leave easily, but the key is to figure out (as much as possible) how or why the enemy gained an entry point. Something produced an agreement in the spiritual realm. Sometimes we grant the enemy access through our own actions and at other times the cause is a generational door. Another way the wrong spirits gain access is because we have come into agreement with a lie, and that lie makes room for the enemy to move in and take up residence.

Satan is known as the father of lies. Nothing that comes out of his mouth can be trusted. Most lies are focused either around some accusation towards God, or some attack on our identity.

It is very important to develop a confidence in knowing who you are in Christ. It is easy to Google a list of scriptures to have on hand and to memorize, so that it gets down on the inside of you. There is no greater weapon against the enemy than the word of God! Understanding your identity, and by gaining a better understanding of scripture allows a person to understand the personal struggles of biblical characters. They too, had to learn to see themselves differently. You are not what you've done. Your identity is not tied to what others have said about you, or whether or not they have given you their stamp of approval. It is also not tied to what you have said about yourself. You are not the sum of your weaknesses and failures. Your identity is based on who you are in Christ, and your position as God's child!

The word of God is powerful and effective at breaking the power of the enemy. Search out scriptures on the topics of lust, temptation, the Father of lies, covetousness, holiness, being a new creation in Christ, and being set free. Post them around your home, office or where ever you feel most likely to be tempted. Those become arrows of truth to fight temptation when the enemy tries to get you off track. Prepare yourself before the attacks come so that you have your weapons ready. Resisting temptation and fighting it with the weapons God has given you is the way of escape. Remember, lust is the temptation to drive a wedge between your relationship with God and others, because it wants to cloak an individual in condemnation, guilt and shame. Recognize where the lie is leading you and take another course of action.

In a previous chapter I shared how I grew up feeling like I was covered with a sense of rejection and shame. Those feelings and attitudes were so ingrained in my belief system that it's been a continuous process of weeding out lies and beliefs that don't reflect who I truly am 'in Christ.' It is this way with all of us. Holy Spirit will transform us and renew our mind until the day we go home to the Lord.

One day quite out of the blue Holy Spirit popped in and began to speak to me about my identity. He told me that even though I had felt rejected all my life, it wasn't a reflection about me personally. He affirmed that I wasn't rejected, but the enemy had an assignment against me from the time I was in my mother's womb. Holy Spirit revealed that Fear and Lust had been assigned to torment me. God also showed me that because of generational sin, those seeds of bitterness, distrust, rebellion, insecurity, anger and torment were things the enemy sowed into me from the very beginning. As Holy Spirit showed me the truth, He also helped me understand that there was nothing wrong with me. I wasn't rejected. The enemy *wanted* me to feel rejection, but it wasn't because I was defective. Satan's lies and deliberate attempts to sabotage my future were behind every attack. As a matter of fact, the Lord began to affirm how much I was loved and accepted. This truth released me from the power of the lie I had believed about myself. After more than 45 years, I got set free! This truth drastically changed the way I saw myself, God and others. This same truth is applicable to you, too. This is just one example how the ministry of the Holy Spirit shatters the power of the lies and leads people into their freedom. We must depend on His help to release revelation!

I used to be so people-conscious that I lived out of fear. It wasn't a conscience awareness of fear or anxiety, but all my perceptions were filtered through that spirit of fear. Fear manifests as insecurity, inferiority (or the feeling of not being able to measure up to the expectations of others), but it also came out as anger. Fear is the root of all anger. A person may have to work at it for a while to identify the lies they have believed, but once the fear is dealt with, the lie is healed and the person is set free. Fear of man causes a fear of embarrassment, and that fear is also the source of deep rooted anger. It is the fear of being shamed and disgraced. This is why relationship with Holy Spirit is so vital to the believer. He can uncover lies and misconceptions and completely renew our mind.

Holy Spirit continues to heal me of very old issues I had forgotten long ago. God recently brought certain memories back to mind. They aren't memories I've wanted to re-live, but I recognize the value of allowing God to deal with them. Several of the situations were from my childhood. Others were from my years as a young adult. Then I realized it was like déjà vu. That familiar pattern had been with me all my life, but I thought it had been broken. In truth, I had received healing in many areas, but it wasn't a complete work. Then I realized that Holy Spirit was connecting more of the dots between old memories, the spirit behind them, and how it still affected some of my beliefs and actions.

The fear of being embarrassed in front of others is rooted in a fear of rejection. I had a very dysfunctional childhood where many things were beyond my control. The adults in my life used shame as a method of discipline, so that's what I learned growing up. Many years later when I finally got saved, I came into a church that I dearly loved, but there was a tendency to use shame as a discipline to motivate people towards right behavior. This just reinforced a very toxic and ungodly belief system. As a child, then again into my adulthood, I didn't have a voice, and felt no sense of safety. God drew the connection between the spirit of fear and how it was manifesting in ways I couldn't readily identify. I realized that the enemy was trying to reproduce the brokenness, fear and shame that I had felt and re-create those same spirits in my family. I have had to work really hard to overcome the old belief system. As God has worked with me, I began to realize the same spirits were at work. That revelation caused me to repent in earnest and gain a change of perspective. Out of that revelation came a prayer strategy to break that generational curse off of my family, as well as gain a sense of freedom and victory.

Every time God has delivered me from something, it wasn't just because I said a particular prayer of renouncement. Yes, God honors those things, but the prayers helped open the door to my understanding so that God could do a deeper work. It can be different for everyone. We all want the quick fix and be set free, but that isn't always the way God works. He wants us to understand what got us in bondage to begin with so that we have the knowledge to stay free and then help share those truths with others. If we refuse to dig deeper then we will only ever get what is just on the surface. Most issues go back a lot further, but it doesn't' have to be a horrendous process of getting healed. The enemy builds things up in our mind so badly that we think we have to be afraid to bring those things to our Father. Why are we so afraid to confront old memories? Why are we afraid to let God speak to us and change our messed up belief system? God is a gentle healer. He is so easy to work with if we just let Him. He wants us to inquire of Him, and invite Him to give us a new perspective. Working with Holy Spirit is imperative so that He can reveal the blind spots. Ask Him to help you understand the root issues of your life. Give Him permission to bring situations to mind so that He can heal your perception of different events in your life. Unhealed wounds are what has given demons permission to remain in people's lives. If we want those spirits to truly lose their grip, we have to recognize how they work so that we can stop cooperating with them.

So many people seem to be cloaked with this mantle of reproach and disgrace. They may or may not be consciously aware of it, but it affects how they feel about themselves. Detachment and defensiveness become a hard outer shell that is constructed to keep people safe. Unfortunately, emotional detachment and disconnectedness never results in a very satisfying life. It also doesn't protect a person from hurt because the person is trapped, alone with their pain, a captive from within their own self-made prison house. If an individual becomes emotionally disconnected then they leave themselves without a sense of comfort. It's like they have burned the bridges to the help that they need in order to become whole again. We are made for relationship. We are made for worship and meaningful communion with God and others. It is so easy to get used to emotional disconnectedness and being alone with our emotions, but that causes grief. It becomes necessary for the individual to be aware of their tendency to isolate themselves. They must work on developing trust with others. Often, the person feels unsure whether or not they can fully trust God. They usually have something in their past where they felt terribly hurt or disappointed, and they felt that God should have protected them.

God has promised to never leave us or forsake us. He is all around us, and He has always been present. The problem is, when people are hurting or alone with their fears, they often can't sense God's presence. They are so focused on their emotions or the turmoil of a certain situation that they focus on those things rather than on seeking God. He is a God of all comfort, but it is hard to comfort someone that is angry, accusing, fearful or so emotionally distraught that they can't hear Him speak. He does surround us with others who can help comfort us. The love, hugs and encouragement from those who know Him are also His way of fulfilling His promise, "I will never leave you or forsake you." He loves us so much He sent His Holy Spirit to live within us. We never have to feel separated from the love of God!

The fear of embarrassment and disgrace is deeply tied to insecurity about identity. The degree to which a person suffers from these fears will ultimately affect their ability to be transparent and real with others, because authenticity requires trust. We do need to learn to trust others, but it's also about placing our trust in God. When we are confident about knowing to whom we belong, then fear loses its grip. Understanding who we are in Christ is the foundational truth to healing and deliverance.

When a person has had their identity attacked repeatedly, it is difficult to recover, especially apart from God's revelation to us. But, it is also an indication of fear and intimidation from the enemy, for he knows that if the person is to get free and realize how much authority they have in Christ, they will do considerable damage to the kingdom of darkness. The very first thing Satan attacked in Jesus was his identity. Satan does the same with each child of God. His goal is to create lies and doubts that cause people to doubt God's ability to keep them safe, protect and provide for them. If they doubt, then they will not trust Him. And, if people don't trust Him, they will stay within their perceived ability to keep themselves safe. Vulnerability always demands an amount of risk. The world needs to hear messages of hope and victory. Others need to hear testimonies of how God has set His people free. They need to know there is hope in Jesus Christ, and it's safe for them to come out of their prison houses. Until we can throw ourselves into the Master's hands and trust Him with our fears, the messages that heal remain trapped inside the messengers.

Shame is such a powerful emotion that it will cause people to reject those who are suffering from it. People have a selfish tendency to want to distance themselves from others who are cloaked in shame. It's the 'shame by association' type of attitude. It's an act of self-preservation when people disassociate themselves from those who they feel others would show disapproval towards. They have this sense that God and others have rejected that person and that they are cursed – so what do they do? They reject them instead of trying to lift their burden and show compassion. Of Jesus it was said,

*"He was despised and forsaken by men, this man of suffering, grief's patient friend. **As if he was a person to avoid, we looked the other way**; he was despised, forsaken, and we took no notice of him. Yet it was our suffering he carried, our pain and distress, our sick-to-the-soul-ness. **We just figured that God had rejected him, that God was the reason he hurt so badly**. But he was hurt because of us; he suffered so. **Our wrongdoing wounded and crushed him.** He endured the breaking that made us whole. <u>The injuries he suffered became our</u>*

healing. _We all have wandered off, like shepherdless sheep, scattered by our aimless striving and endless pursuits; the Eternal One laid on him, this silent sufferer, the sins of us all._" (Isaiah 53:3-6 VOICE)

Jesus bore our shame – _and others have born our shame_, not just their own, but the rejection from people that have deemed them rejected and despised members of society. The reality is, many of those who have been rejected are the ones who carry the anointed messages that will restore hope, healing and deliverance. You might not have thought you needed those people, but you do. We all do. They are the ones that old the keys that others need.

Many of the trials we face are because people fail to understand their identity in Christ. From the day we were born, Satan has attempted to remake us into his image and forge a new identity. When we get saved, Holy Spirit begins to uncover the lies we've believed. He shows us truth so that we can understand how to believe God for our promises, and learn to exercise our dominion.

Jesus' disciples struggled with this concept, too. Although they were with the Lord day and night, hearing His teaching on the kingdom and watching Him work miracles, it still took them a long time to realize that He was giving them

His kingdom. A proper understanding of identity is to realize that it can only be understood through a personal, intimate relationship with the Lord. It is allowing Holy Spirit to reveal both who we are and to whom we belong. It is the revelation of our Father's love and acceptance that makes us fearless in the face of the enemy. Before the foundation of the world He chose us to be adopted as sons and daughters, holy and blameless, secure in His love and acceptance.[46] That knowledge builds confidence on the inside of us. God's perfect love casts out the fear of man and the torment of insecurity.[47] God's love casts out the enemies of intimacy and barriers to trust. His love makes us brave! To know one's identity is to have confidence in knowing that nothing can truly harm us. We are secure in Him. And that is what stabilizes our faith, knowing that we have dominion over the enemy.

Psalm 27:1 is a Psalm of David. When we know our identity and feel secure in it, like David we can say,

"The LORD is my light and my salvation--so why should I be afraid? The LORD is my fortress, protecting me from danger, so why should I tremble?" (NLT)

---

[46] Ephesians 1:4-6.

[47] 1 John 4:18

I understand why, when dealing with sensitive personal information like this, people would rather choose anonymity rather than vulnerability and transparency; however, opting for self-preservation does not seem the proper course of action if we are to help set the captives free. It was said of Jesus that for the joy set before Him He endured the agony of His soul. Jesus laid down his life for us and calls us friends.

"This is My commandment, that you love one another as I loved you. Greater love has no one than this: to lay down one's life for one's friends." (John 15:12,13)

"For whoever wants to save his life will lose it, but whoever loses his life for My sake will save it." (Luke 9:24)

Daily we are faced with the same choice to pick up our cross and die to ourselves. It is the high calling of Christ Jesus. We can either choose to hold our testimonies in captivity and only share the parts we are comfortable with, or trust the Lord with our reputation and share our stories with others in hope that they, too, will discover the needed information that leads them out of darkness and into freedom.

So many people are intimidated when it comes to

sharing their weaknesses with others. They fear how others will perceive them. Yet scripture reminds us that when we are weak, that is when Christ shows His strength in us. If that fear crops up, remember that it is simply another lie from the enemy, attempting to seduce us away from the truth, and to hinder us from reaching others. The truth is found in 2 Cor. 12:9,10.

"My grace is sufficient for you, for My power is perfected in weakness." Therefore I will boast all the more gladly in my weaknesses, so that the power of Christ may rest on me. That is why, for the sake of Christ, I delight in weaknesses, in insults, in hardships, in persecutions, in difficulties. For when I am weak, then I am strong."

When we are vulnerable before others and honest about our own weaknesses and struggles, it makes us feel naked and insecure. The Lord showed me in a dream a very different reality. He showed me that when we are transparent, we feel unsafe and vulnerable to being attacked; however, that is when we are actually completely surrounded by His armor. It's so secure it's like being inside a bullet proof, armor plated vehicle. We are actually completely safe because our transparency leaves the enemy nothing to work with. All his weapons are taken away. He has nothing to use against us. And, in that place of humility, vulnerability and transparency, that is when the power of God rests upon us and allows our story to become healing and breakthrough to others. That is when, once again, we can stand before God and take comfort in His presence. When we put our confidence in God, we can stand before Him naked and unashamed.

CHAPTER TEN
PRACTICAL STEPS TO DELIVERANCE

The most practical advice I can give someone else that wants to know more about deliverance is that it must begin with them. In order to guide someone else through the process, a person must be familiar with it. One cannot understand what it takes to get free if they haven't walked through it. There are some key foundational issues that must be worked out in a person's life before they attempt to guide someone else through their process.

Deliverance ministry is not for the novice. It is for those that are mature and have experience being delivered from bondage and have made a commitment to living a sanctified life. While anyone can pray for others, it is also having a proper sense of understanding about spiritual warfare issues. The single most important factor is understanding your identity in Christ. A person that understands their identity will stand firm in their authority, but be led by a heart of humility and compassion. Without compassion for those who are suffering, a sense of pride and judgment will be reflected that can end up wounding others. You are God's co-worker in the ministry of reconciliation.[48] As such, it is very important to have purity in your lifestyle, and to make sure that you have also taken care to close doors to the enemy through prayers of renouncement before you attempt to take authority over evil spirits. One should not engage in direct confrontation with spirits of darkness unless they know that they have taken care of sin in their own life. Never go to war with open doors that will allow the enemy to come back and exploit something in your own life.

The second most important thing is to be filled with the Holy Spirit, for it is the gifts of the Spirit that minister healing and freedom to others. Jesus counseled His disciples to wait for the power of the Holy Spirit to come upon them in order to make them effective witnesses to the rest of the world. [49] The truth of the gospel should always be accompanied with signs of God's power to heal and deliver because that is what witnesses to the truth of His kingdom. [50] Ministry must

---

[48] 2 Cor. 5:17-20; 6:1

[49] Acts 1:8

[50] 1 Cor. 2:4; 1 Cor. 4:20

flow out of relationship with Jesus Christ and His Holy Spirit, and we must be dependent upon Him to reveal the source of people's issues. It is His truth that sets captives free.

Deliverance ministry works best when it is done as a team. Jesus sent the disciples out in twos because it is more effective. The manifestations of the Holy Spirit operate differently depending on the individual. Therefore it makes sense that you want people that function in the ministry gifts. [51]

- The word of wisdom
- The word of knowledge
- The gift of faith
- The gift of healing
- The working of miracles
- The gift of prophecy
- The gift of discerning of spirits
- Different types of tongues
- Interpretation of tongues

The prayer team should pray together first, if at all possible. Fasting is also suggested. You never know when you will encounter a stubborn spirit. [52]

---

[51] 1 Cor. 12:8-10

[52] Matt.17:21; Mark 9:29

Whenever possible, try to evaluate the person coming for ministry to see if they are genuinely ready to do what it takes on their part for healing and deliverance to take place. Sometimes people just want others to listen to their complaints but they are not ready to be obedient to God. That is where it is very good to use wisdom and discernment so that the enemy doesn't just waste your time and wear you out.

Ask the person if they can identify a time in their past when they first started experiencing the problem. Questions such as, "Where in your past does this feel familiar?" or "What do you feel, see, hear, or sense God showing you about this memory/problem/issue?" Invite Holy Spirit to speak and reveal a different perspective on the situation. Remember, it's not so much about what the individual might remember, because **sometimes the problem they are having is not related to one of their memories**. It might have originated from something concerning their parents, grandparents or another ancestor that they have no way of knowing the real source of the issue. Ask Holy Spirit to reveal what **He knows** about the situation, then pray over what He reveals. It is important for the person to renounce whatever sins were involved as well as declare that they are breaking any agreements or covenants in the spirit realm that might have been formed with demonic entities.

Encourage the person not to be timid about making these declarations. God has not given them a spirit of fear, but of power, love and a sound mind. [53] The righteous should be as bold as a lion. They need to be encouraged to rise up in strength and take back their dominion.

Be prepared for manifestations of evil spirits. Warn the individual as well as the prayer team not to be alarmed, and not to give in to fear, emotional outbursts, anger, or other such manifestations. The person you're trying to help may feel like running away from the session. Sometimes that spirit will try to get them to avoid coming altogether. They sense what's coming. Let them know this is the enemy trying to avoid being cast out and they should not give in to it. Other manifestations of demons leaving can include things such as:

- Yawning
- Belching
- Crying
- Sighing
- Coughing
- Blowing out of the mouth forcibly
- Screaming or shrieking

---

[53] 2 Tim. 1:7

- Feeling sick

Sometimes people feel demons leave and other times there is no outward sign at all. The person should feel better afterward. Many people describe feeling lighter, like a heavy weight has been lifted off their shoulders.

Minister to each person individually. If a husband and wife come together, or sometimes a parent and child, ask if it is ok to minister to them separately. Obviously, if it is a young child the parent should be present. An older child may feel more comfortable without their parent, depending on the nature of the issue. Parents and spouses can sometimes have their own agenda that can derail the ministry of the Holy Spirit. If they just want prayer for a general issue that is different than those coming for deliverance. In addition, sometimes one of the parties may feel somewhat apprehensive or awkward in front of the other, and perhaps not disclose information vital to the ministry process.

Ministry teams should have both male and female members available to minister. The variety of gifts in different individuals are welcomed, but a man should minister to a man, or at least be available in the team, and women should minister to women.

Before you begin, try to assess the nature of th problem. Ask the person if they know what the problem is, or if they can summarize what they think may be the issue. Most often, they will be describing circumstances or other negative situations. This is known as the fruit. Trace the fruit back to the root. You need to be able to identify the root system that is operating in the person's life. As they explain, take note of things that could be open doors for curses to be activated in their life, such as divorce or broken covenants, addictions, involvement in the occult or other religions, a past history of visiting tarot card readers or fortune tellers, playing with a Ouija board or other occult games, involvement in yoga or New Age practices, unforgiveness or a root of bitterness, speaking against others (the sin of slander, gossip or murder with the mouth), abortion (releases a spirit of abortion) – this manifests as starts & stops with relationships, employment, living conditions, etc.. Both slander and abortion are equivalent to the sin of murder. That releases a curse of wandering (the curse of Cain) which affects stability. It produces starts and stops in the person's life. These are just a few things to remember as the person shares some background history. If they mention any of these things, lead them in a prayer of repentance to renounce the sins of their ancestors as well as themselves. Unforgiveness issues are also quite common. The individual must forgive from the heart. This area of counseling may ile to help them see the value of meaningful Many people will agree to say the words ' I _____', but their heart is not really involved in the process. This often leaves the issue unresolved where a root of bitterness can take hold in the person. God wants genuine repentance. Jesus said we must forgive from our heart.[54] If the person has difficulty making their confession genuine, then have them fast and pray before proceeding. If they are stuck on an unforgiveness issue, demons have a right to stay and the rest of the session will probably not be effective. Have them come back after fasting and praying through the situation. Fasting helps soften the heart and allow the root to come out. Then you will be able to proceed to different issues.

If a person is secretly in agreement with the attitude or sin, wait until they have a change of heart.

One of the most important things to do for the person is to share with them about being filled with the baptism of the Holy Spirit. It fills the void where the enemy had taken up residence. Scripture tells us that a house swept clean is in danger of being occupied by evil spirits – and more of them if

---

[54] Matthew 6:15; Matt. 18:35

the house is not filled with God. [55]

"When an unclean spirit goes out of a man, it passes through dry places seeking rest, but finds none. Then it says, 'I will return to my house from which I came.' And when it comes, it finds it empty, swept, and put in order." (Matt. 12:33-34)

Please, *do not* leave people vulnerable and empty where the enemy can just come in all over again. Explain about the beautiful gift of speaking in tongues and how it is there to edify the believer, and help them overcome in Christ. It is negligence not to offer that gift that can help them have the power they need to live a sanctified life. Ask them if they wish to receive this blessing. Ask them to invite Holy Spirit to baptize them in their heavenly language, then lay hands on them and pray. Release the living waters to flow from within them according to John 7:38. This is also how the gifts of the Spirit are released, through the dynamic, life-giving power of God.

There will always be variances, of course, in any sort of personal ministry. It is important to do things decently and in order, allowing each person on the ministry team to share what God is showing them about the individual, without

---

[55] Matt.12:33,34

causing the person to feel overwhelmed. Do only what you can do comfortably in the time allotted. Some additional sessions may be necessary.

The following prayer is lengthy but thorough in helping a person to close doors to the enemy and also cut off generational curses. Please feel free to use it as a guide to seeking God and discussing the various issues with Him. Ask Holy Spirit to highlight anything specific in your background, or in your bloodline. Take time to linger over the various areas and communicate with Holy Spirit. This should be viewed as a starting point. Some people experience immediate breakthrough, while it's a slower process in others. That's ok. Let the prayer begin its work.

BREAKTHROUGH PRAYER:

Dear Heavenly Father,

I come to You on behalf of myself and all those in my ancestral line that came before me. I ask for Your forgiveness for our sins, and I acknowledge that many of us never asked for Jesus Christ to be our Lord and Savior. Many of us committed sins and trespasses in rebellion to Your ways.

Father, I also come to you as a citizen of the United States, and I ask You to forgive the sins of our forefathers. I ask You to forgive the sins of those that pioneered and settled this land, and the pagan practices, cultures and traditions brought in from foreign lands. Forgive, I pray, our presidential and political leaders that broke treaties and treacherously removed the boundary lines of Native Americans and others to claim them as their own.

Forgive all those in my family line as well as those who founded our nation and settled the land for making slaves of other races and nationalities; for causing others to feel overcome with jealousy, fear, anger and desire vengeance against those who treated them wrongfully.

Forgive us for the grief we caused, the injustices and the bloodshed. Forgive us for broken covenants, vows and agreements and for the curses that came as a result of those actions. Although I may not have personally taken part in these sins, I understand that there is a need to recognize the sins of those that came before us and I ask for the blood of Jesus to atone for these things so that we may be cleansed of all these unrighteous acts. Please allow all those that have been affected by this generational root of bitterness, grief and poverty now find the grace to forgive, even generations of mistreatment and injustices.

Father, You said that if I would humble myself, pray and seek Your face...If I would turn and repent from my wicked ways, You said You would forgive my sins. Whether other family members or myself have partaken of these sins knowingly or unknowingly, I ask Your forgiveness and I renounce:

All spirits of fear, the fear of man that brings a snare, self-pity, insecurity, and inferiority. Forgive me for the need to control or manipulate others out of a sense of fear, insecurity or inferiority. Forgive me for not trusting in your provision or your timing, and for failing to rest in Your love. Father, I thank you that Your perfect love casts out all fear according to 1 John 4:18. I come out of agreement with the spirit of fear and command it to leave me now, in the name and authority of Jesus Christ. Let the curse of fear and anxiety be broken now in Jesus name.

I renounce bitterness, jealousy, strife, anger, hatred, profanity, gossip, lying, slander and murder with the mouth. I repent for holding on to bitterness that comes from being hurt, mistreated or injustice that has occurred towards myself or others in my family. I renounce the spirit of Cain, which is a murderous spirit. I come out of agreement with these spirits and repent for my judgments against others. I command bitterness, jealousy, strife, anger, hatred, profanity, gossip, lying, slander and rage to leave me now in the name and authority of Jesus Christ. I willingly forgive all those that have hurt and offended me, from my heart. Let all curses of rejection, wandering and instability be broken now in Jesus name.

Forgive me and those in my family for any sins of hard heartedness, being critical or condemning, or showing lack of compassion towards others in their time of need. Forgive me and those in my family for turning a blind eye towards those in need and withholding good when it was in our power to help. Father, please let the hardness of my heart be changed. Let Your compassion fill my heart. Let the curse of greed that produces poverty be broken now in Jesus name.

I renounce the sin of abortion which is premeditated murder. Father, forgive me and anyone in my family for shedding innocent blood. Please let the spirit of abortion be broken off of my life. Let the blood of Jesus cover this sin and close the door to the curse in Jesus name.

I renounce all spirits of heaviness that bring depression, mental illness, obsessive compulsive disorders, schizophrenia, suicide, bi-polar disease and grief. I renounce *the spirits of insanity, unbelief, double-mindedness, the cares of this world and all things that would give me give me divided loyalties in my heart and mind towards God. I renounce every seed that Satan has sown into my heart and mind that would cause divided loyalties and weaken my convictions towards Jesus Christ. I come out of agreement with the spirits of insanity, unbelief and doublemindedness and I command them to leave me now, in the name and authority of Jesus Christ. Let the curse of unbelief and double-mindedness be broken now in Jesus name.*

I renounce all compulsive behavior and all addictions rooted in fear, rejection, or anxiety. I come out of agreement with spirits of compulsion, fear, rejection and anxiety. I command them to leave me now in the name and authority of Jesus Christ. Let the curse of all mental illness be broken now in Jesus name.

I renounce and forsake unforgiveness, including unforgiveness towards myself, retaliation, and vengeance. Forgive me, Lord, for any time that me or my family members have sown seeds of discord or caused pain to others. I repent for sins of judging or rejecting others, withholding love, acceptance or forgiveness. Forgive me for failing to show love, mercy, grace or compassion. Let the judgments I have spoken about others bear no more fruit in my life or theirs. Let the power of negative words I have spoken be broken now and I ask you to please release me from reaping judgment into my own life, in Jesus name.

I renounce and forsake spirits of self-hatred, self-rejection, unloving spirits, guilt, condemnation and shame. Father I thank you for your forgiveness. Your word says there is therefore now no condemnation for those who are in Christ Jesus. I come out of agreement with the spirits of self-hatred, self-rejection, unloving spirits, guilt, condemnation and shame, and command them to leave me now. Let all shame and condemnation be broken off my life now in Jesus name.

I renounce and forsake spirits of rejection and abandonment, all lying spirits and command them to leave me at once. I thank you Father that I am not rejected; I am accepted in the Beloved. I come out of agreement with spirits of rejection and abandonment and command them to leave me in the name and authority of Jesus Christ. Your word says You will never leave me or forsake me. I am loved and accepted according to Your word in Ephesians 1:6. Let the curse of abandonment be broken now in Jesus name.

I renounce and forsake all soul ties to illegitimate spiritual fathers or spiritual leaders, religious attitudes, and spirits of legalism, disrespect, self-righteousness, pride, , pretense, hypocrisy, masquerade, prejudice, controlling behaviors, manipulation, imposing my will on others, racism, disobedience, independence, critical spirits, arrogance, vain and judgmental attitudes. I come out of agreement with religious witchcraft, hypocrisy, pride, pretense, masquerade, control, guilt, manipulation and self-righteousness and I command them to leave me now, in the name and authority of Jesus Christ. Let the curse associated with these spirits be broken now in Jesus name.

Forgive me for not being able to separate the sin of those that have hurt me from them as human beings that have also been hurt and used by the enemy to hurt others. Forgive me for rebellion to authority and the times when I have not honored nor shown respect to those in authority, parents, spouses or others. Forgive me for not humbling myself or apologizing when I should have done so. I come out of agreement with the lies and the spirit of rebellion, insubordination and pride, and I command them to leave me now. Let every curse associated with these spirits be broken now in Jesus name.

I renounce and repent for all broken covenants, unfulfilled vows and promises, betrayal and divorce. I ask you to forgive me for any way that my actions may have provoked jealousy or pain in others. I pray that You heal any wounds in others that I may have caused. Let the curse of miscarriage, fertility problems, jealousy, and broken relationships be broken now in Jesus name.

I ask You to forgive me for making agreements with the wrong people. Please disentangle me and release me from ungodly covenants, vows, and unrighteous agreements. I ask You to break me free from agreements and relationships where I am yoked with things of the kingdom of darkness, evil and wrong relationships, in Jesus name.

I repent of all sexual sins. I renounce and divorce all spirits of lust, covetousness and witchcraft. I renounce and forsake all soul ties to former lovers, and any soul ties that were formed through trauma, pain, shame, abuse, deep disappointment and broken vows. Let the fragmented pieces of those people's soul return to them, and let the fragmented pieces of my soul return to me. Please heal the fragmentation in my soul and spirit. I renounce the perverse spirit. I renounce and forsake incubus and succubus spirits, ungodly fantasies, spirits of voyeurism, perverse sexual practices and homosexuality. I ask You, Holy Spirit, to purify my eye gate, my senses and desires. Help me be diligent to guard these places of my heart and mind so that the enemy cannot use these things as a temptation to ensnare me. I come out of agreement with these spirits and command them to leave me now, in the name and authority of the Lord Jesus Christ. I ask You, Holy Spirit, to help me come back to my senses. I thank You, Father, that you have created me to be holy and blameless according to Ephesians 1:4. Let every curse associated with these things be broken now in Jesus name.

I renounce and forsake all false gods, masters and all evil inheritances that have come through family line. I renounce African religions, the false practices and traditions of other religions and their saints, patrons and patronesses and spirit guides. I renounce and repent, on behalf of myself and my ancestors for any covenants or agreements made with the false god known as Olodumare, the spirits known as Papa Legba, Obatala, Oya, Oshun, Osain, Chango, Oggun and Yemmaya. I declare there is no other God except for Jesus Christ and I break any connections or agreements that have been made through candle burning, calling on the names of false gods or saints, and invoking their assistance. I come out of agreement with these familiar spirits and I divorce all gods and masters of various names. I command them to leave me now in the name and authority of Jesus Christ. Let every curse associated with these things be broken now in Jesus name.

I renounce the demonic spirits of hoodoo, voodoo, Satanism, and all spirits of witchcraft and magic in the name of Jesus Christ. I renounce the god of the graveyard, Baron Samedi, and the loa Maman Bridgitte, and all gods, amulets and practices of Haitian voodoo. I renounce all witchcraft practices of juju. I come out of agreement with any covenants and invitations of these spirits made by myself or my ancestors and I command them to leave me now in the name and authority of Jesus Christ. Let every curse associated with these spirits be broken now in Jesus name.

I renounce and repent for any involvement with secret societies and the ungodly covenants they demand. (If you know which ones are involved in your family history, name them).I renounce and forsake all pledges, oaths and involvement with Freemasonry, lodges, societies or crafts by my ancestors and myself. I renounce and forsake all false gods, false doctrines, unholy communion and abominations. I renounce and forsake the Luciferian doctrine; I renounce and forsake the oaths spoken to pledge loyalties to man or idol that violated the commands of God and conscience. I renounce all false masters associated with Freemasons, Shriners, Mormonism, Paganism, the Klu Klux Klan and other lodges and secret societies. I renounce and forsake the false god Allah. I renounce and forsake all words and phrases used as secret codes and I break agreement with all curses that were once agreed to be placed upon any and all family members, including myself and future generations. I come out of agreement with these covenants and evil spirits, and command them to leave me now in the name and authority of Jesus Christ. Let every curse associated with these abominations be broken now in Jesus name.

I renounce all lies and false teaching that blinds me to truth and mocks and resists God. I renounce all ungodly symbols that connect me to false teaching, false gods, ungodly alliances and pagan symbolism. I accept and receive no inheritance from evil sources, only that which my heavenly Father permits and allows. Let all evil inheritances be broken off of me and my family. Father, forgive me and my ancestors for resisting truth and resisting Your authority. Holy Spirit, I ask you to forgive me for grieving You and mocking the things of God. I renounce the spirits of mocking, scoffing, the deaf and dumb spirit, the spirit of blindness and all mind blinding spirits. I renounce the anti-Christ spirit and the spirit of pride. Let the power of Leviathan be broken off of my life. I come out of agreement with these spirits and command them to leave me now in the name and authority of Jesus Christ. Let every curse associated with these sins be broken now in Jesus name.

Lord, let there be a release of every curse that has come

against me or my generational line as a result of these things. I decree a cancellation of every form of witchcraft and curse that has resulted from my involvement or that of my generational line. I ask You, Lord Jesus, to come and deliver me and my family from all demonic spirits that have come as a result of a curse. I ask that You restore all the years that the enemy has stolen according to your promise in Joel 2:25,26. Let the blessings that have been held back, stolen and hidden by the enemy be released into my hands now, in Jesus name. Let all demonic attachments be severed from me and my family line, both in the heavenly places as well as in the earthly realm. I declare that every seed that was sown by Satan in order to perpetuate a curse or cause myself or someone else in my family line to reject my heavenly Father, the Lord Jesus Christ and Holy Spirit must now shrivel and die immediately. Jesus, I give You permission to change what You know needs to change in my life and to convict me if I resist your Holy Spirit.

Father, I repent for these sins on behalf of me and my family to the tenth generation back. I thank You for Your forgiveness and cleansing of these sins. I declare that when I am tested, the Spirit of God will arise within me and bring me into a place of victory. I give You permission in advance of any situation I may encounter that You and Your Holy Spirit may change my actions, words and responses so that I honor You. Please reign and rule over my emotions.

Enemy, according to the scripture in James 4:7, as I am now submitted to God, you must flee from me. I command you to take everything that you have put on me, everything that you have tormented me with, every sickness and GO! I command you to pay restitution at no less than a 7-fold return, according to Proverbs 6:31 in every place that you have brought poverty, defeat, robbery, or death and destruction.

Today I declare that the enemy is defeated where I am concerned. You are my Master, my Lord and my Savior. Please come with Your Holy Spirit and heal my mind, my emotions, my thoughts, my confession and my core beliefs. Please heal my trust issues with you and others. Please heal the issues related to my past, my present and my future. Heal my hope, my faith and my love. Heal any areas of grief, heaviness, unbelief, and let the renewed mind of Christ be strengthened and formed in me each and every day. Thank You for releasing into me a spirit of Faith, a spirit of Obedience, the spirit of Adoption, the spirit of Revelation and Truth. Now tell me Lord, what I need to do as an act of faith that will release my breakthrough. Confirm it and convict me that I will not neglect to do whatever You tell me to do. Thank You for eternal life, health, and victory, and for restoring my life and my future, in Jesus' precious name, Amen.

In my attempts to assist certain individuals from African descent, I have noticed that there are some additional things that may be not specifically addressed in the Breakthrough Prayer. Sometimes there are things in a person's ancestry that need a more targeted approach, such as those who have specific forms of African, Cuban or Haitian occultism involved in their ancestry. It is also helpful if a person has spent an extended period of time into some of these places, to insure that some of those spirits do not cling to people when they come back. I will include this prayer also, because of the growing number of those involved or have a history with Voodoo, Hoodoo and other occult religious practices. Those in the African culture often have a history of witchcraft and sorcery in their bloodline. Rituals are often performed when a new child enters the family, and sometimes the rituals are performed later in childhood as a rite of passage or indoctrination into shamanism and witchcraft. This prayer is to break those ungodly alliances and demonic attachments.

Dear Heavenly Father,

I seek Your help, the help that is only available to me

through Jesus Christ, the blood of the lamb, and His Holy Spirit. I desperately want to be cleansed from demonic spirits, unbroken curses and familiar spirits that have been a part of my life, through my family members, from even before my birth. I ask You, Jesus Christ, Lord of all, to be my Lord and Savior. I ask You to cleanse me from all unrighteousness and set me free.

I repent for any way that I have knowingly or unknowingly given place to demonic spirits and allowed them to access my life. I renounce the sins of my parents, grandparents, and other ancestors that have participated in witchcraft, all forms of sorcery and occultism. This day I divorce the enemy, Satan, and all other false gods and religions.

I renounce and divorce the enemy, Satan, all anti-Christ spirits, and any evil spirit that may have been called into my life.

I renounce the following spirits : Baal, Python, Lucifer, Jezebel, the spirit of Babylon and whoredoms, Bast, Ma'at, Nehebka, Seth, Isis, Zeus, Leviathan, Rahab, Beelzebub, Belial, Molech, Chemosh, Baphomet, Abaddon and all destroyer spirits, Lamia, Lilith, Lilu and all Lilin spirits. I renounce all vampire spirits.

I renounce all sun gods, moon gods, gods to the stars and planets;

I renounce all water spirits, mermaids and mermen spirits, all spirits that dwell beneath the sea, including sea snakes and the serpents of Sheol;

I renounce all unclean spirits;

I renounce the false god known as the god of fortresses;

I renounce bush and forest spirits, wind, sky and fire spirits;

I renounce high level ruling spirits known as Ascended Masters;

I renounce the spirits of Santeria, Lukumi, African gods and all familiar spirits associated with rituals, prayers, customs and traditions. I renounce the African spirits known as Olodumare, Papa Legba, Obatala, Oya, Oshun, Osain, Chango, Oggun and Yemmaya, in the name of Jesus Christ.

I renounce the demonic waters of initiation into the occult known as Adukrom Nsu;

I renounce the god of the graveyard, Baron Samedi, and the loa Maman Bridgitte, and all gods, amulets and practices of Haitian voodoo;

I renounce all witchcraft practices of juju;

I renounce the false god known as the Grand Master;

I renounce all Loas, mediums and familiar spirits, ungodly priests, priestesses, sorcerers and wizards.

I renounce fear, self-will, lust, control and confusion.

I break every ungodly covenant, oath and vow that may have been spoken by myself or any of my ancestors, even being dedicated to Satan from before my birth. I know that this is forbidden by Your word. Lord Jesus, please let me be released from any ungodly alliances, covenants, or legally binding treaties that were enacted between me, my family, and demonic spirits.

I renounce African and cultural witchcraft, Yoruba traditions, shamans, witch doctors, their rituals and Voodoo that have been practiced by my ancestors. I want nothing to do with those practices, rituals, and traditions and I renounce them all, in Jesus name.

I renounce divination and conjuring of all familiar spirits of the dead and those that my ancestors and family members have participated in. I renounce all soul ties to familiar and familial protectors, spirit guides, scribes and messengers, diviners and ungodly priests, false fathers and mothers, and those known as babalawo.

I renounce all inanimate objects used for divining purposes, including casting of chains. Lord Jesus, I ask that You break every ungodly chain that has tied me to these things that I am now renouncing.

I renounce all animal and material sacrifices made on my behalf or those in my family line. I renounce all human involvement for the sake of divining information, the use of familiar spirits, spirit guides, and false gods. I renounce all blood that was shed from any source that was tied to my life through the use of occult practices. I renounce all herbalists and root workers that concocted medicines, potions, magic and incantations used in Ayajo.

I repent and renounce for any participation of myself or those in my family line in the indoctrination, apprenticeship, spiritual journey, rituals or rites of passage of myself or others into occult practices.

I renounce all lying, devious, deceptive and manipulative spirits that were inherited as a curse.

I renounce the spirit of fear, suspicion, rejection, loneliness, inferiority, insecurity, poverty, death and hell that have come into my life.

I renounce the spirit of abandonment, unloving spirits, guilt and condemnation.

I renounce all spirits of infirmity.

Father God, Lord Jesus and Holy Spirit,

I want nothing to do with any of these spirits or their ungodly practices. This day I divorce the enemy and all false gods that have been a part of my life, whether through inherited curses, the sins of my ancestors or my own involvement. Please forgive me and those in my family line. Please wash us clean from this iniquity and let the blood of Jesus cover our sins, and close the doors to the enemy. I ask you to cleanse me from all unrighteousness according to Your word in 1 John 1:9. You said if I confessed my sins, You were able and just to forgive them and cleanse me from this unrighteousness. I submit to Your Lordship, Jesus, and the authority of Your Holy Spirit. You are the only God for me! I will not serve any other God but You! I ask You to restore my life, my health, my finances, my well being, good, healthy and godly relationships, and bless me the way you want me to be blessed.

Father, I forgive my family members for the hurt they have caused me. I forgive them for releasing curses in my life. I ask You to bless them with revelation and understanding of the error of their ways so that they can find their salvation and deliverance in You, Jesus. Please heal their minds, set their hearts free, and take good care of them. I release them into your hands.

Now, confident that I am forgiven of my own sins, I take the authority that You have given me, and I declare:

According to Revelation 12:9,the dragon, that old serpent called Satan and the devil has been cast out of me, and all his dark angels with him .

In the name and authority of Jesus Christ, I loose myself from all punishing, tormenting and vengeful spirits assigned to my life that would perpetuate a curse.

In the name and authority of Jesus Christ, I declare Him

only to be my shield, protector, guardian, and refuge.

I command every demonic chain to be severed from my life in the name of Jesus.

(This next part is included for for those seeking future mates or if you are praying for your children's future spouse).

I declare that death and hell no longer have the right to advance against my life or any future children or family members I may have. Father, I pray that you prepare the heart and life of my future spouse (As well as my children's spouses) to also be educated and informed about generational curses. Prepare him/her/them now also, to be cleansed from the iniquity of her bloodlines. Help us/them to be well prepared for one another, and I trust You to bring us together when we are adequately prepared for one another. Let us together raise a family without inherited generational curses, and train our/their children in the ways of the Lord.

I command every demonic spirit on assignment over my life to return to the place that Jesus made for you. Do not come back, I want nothing to do with you and I resist you! According to James 4:7 you must now flee from me, my home and everything that pertains to me. Get out in Jesus name!!

Let the curse over my home, myself and my family, and all that pertains to us be broken now, in Jesus name. I thank You, Father, for allowing us to receive Your restoration and the blessings that have been held back. I ask that Your Holy Spirit fill me with love, truth, wisdom, might, a spirit of understanding and enable me to live according to Your commands. Let the ruach, the breath of God come into me now, according to John 20:22 where You breathed on Your disciples and they received the breath of God. In Jesus name, Amen.

Conclusion

Shame is not our portion. It's not our future. God has promised that He has a good plan for our lives, to give us a future and a hope. It doesn't matter what others have said about us. Other people's opinions are not truth, and their opinion has absolutely no bearing upon our value. Only God can determine our worth. **What matters is what we believe about God and about ourselves.** His promise to us is also found in Isaiah 61:7.

"Many called you disgraced and defiled and said that shame should be your share of things. Yet you suffered doubly and lived in disgrace; So double will be your share, and with joy everlasting."

His word also promises that blessing awaits us when we are cleansed from the things that bring defilement.[56] The

---

[56] Ezekiel 36:33-36

ruins of our lives will be rebuilt, and we will flourish. Scripture tells us that in a twinkling of an eye we will be changed from one state of being to another. We don't have to wait until that final day. You are one declaration away from a breakthrough. Healing is only one revelation away. Your very next prayer could be just the one that releases you from your chains and brings you through a new level of transformation. May your faith carry you beyond every barrier and into His loving arms!

ABOUT THE AUTHOR

Laura Gagnon is blessed with the gift of understanding God's restorative work through her own personal experiences. She knows first-hand the power of God's compassion, grace and mercy. Through her prophetic insights, teaching and revelation, God has led her to influence many people into a restored relationship with Jesus Christ. Once bound by bitterness, witchcraft, lust, shame and fear, she now helps others find their way out of spiritual oppression. Laura stands on the promises of God and encourages others in an elevated expectation of the miraculous, boldly declaring the gift of His life. Laura has authored several other books including *Healing the Heart of a Woman, Prayers for Impossible Situations* and *Healing the Heart of a Nation*. She is co-author of her husband's book, *Room to Grow*, and also writes for her blog, *"Beyond the Barriers."* Contact Laura Gagnon at xpectamiracle@yahoo.com.

Made in the USA
San Bernardino, CA
05 August 2018